D0095967

"To those who are suffering, or struggling, or trying to make their everyday, ordinary way in the world more extraordinary through a conscious living of their days, Karen Wyatt has penned a poignant epistle. This is not a dark account of the dying. It is a daring look at what it means to be fully alive. With the care of a physician and the soul of a spiritual seeker, Wyatt takes her readers on a journey to their most authentic selves. Part field guide, part confession of faith, *What Really Matters* is at once a tender reflection on our shared humanity and an urgent call to action in each particular life. Listen deep and take these lessons into yourself wholly. You hold in your hands a legacy of lives with the power to transform your own."

Reverend Tammy D. Bell
author of *NOW! Life On Purpose*

What Really Matters

What Really Matters

*7 Lessons for Living
from the
Stories of the Dying*

Karen M. Wyatt, MD

Sunroom Studios
Silverthorne, CO

This edition published by Sunroom Studios
For information address Sunroom Studios, Silverthorne, CO

First Edition

ISBN 978-0-9826855-2-5

Library of Congress Cataloging-in-Publication Data

Wyatt, Karen M.
  What really matters : 7 lessons for living from the stories of the dying /
Karen M. Wyatt. -- 1st ed.
    p. cm.
  Summary: "A hospice physician relates stories about the end-of-life
spiritual wisdom of several dying patients and their families in order to
offer seven profound lessons to change one's perspective toward suffering,
life, and death"--Provided by publisher.
  ISBN 978-0-9826855-2-5(pbk. : alk. paper)
  1. Death--Psychological aspects. 2. Terminally ill--Psychology.
  3. Spiritual life. 4. Conduct of life. I. Title.
  BF789.D4W93 2011
  155.9'37--dc22
                    2011014092

Manufactured in the United States of America

10 9 8 7 6 5 4 3 2 1

For my mother who taught me to see the beauty of the garden;
And for my father who taught me to reach for the stars.

CONTENTS

Acknowledgments   xi
Introduction   xiii

PART I *The Groundwork*

Preparing for the Lessons   3

PART II *The Lessons*

Lesson 1 Suffering: Embrace Your Difficulties   15
    The Vision of an Artist   16

Lesson 2 Love: Let Your Heart Be Broken   27
    Mother and Child   28

Lesson 3 Forgiveness: Hold No Resentments   47
    Brotherly Love   48

Lesson 4 Paradise: Dwell in the Present Moment   67
    The Student Desk   68

Lesson 5 Purpose: Manifest Your Highest Potential   85
    A Vessel of Love   86

Lesson 6 Surrender: Let Go of Expectations   103
    The Face of the Divine   104

Lesson 7 Impermanence: Face Your Fear   121
    In the Presence of a Yogi   122

PART III *The Harvest*

Living the Lessons   143
    The Hollyhock Miracles   144

Acknowledgments

My heartfelt thanks goes out to the many people who played a role in the completion of this book, either by offering their direct support and expertise or through their silent prayers for me as I labored over this task of love. To Mary Langford, "Author Concierge" from Mark Victor Hansen's *Wealthy Writer's Wisdom* course: thank you for believing in my book when it was in its earliest stages and offering me the encouragement I needed to keep moving forward. My gratitude also extends to my editor Jeanne McCafferty for working with diligence and devotion to ensure that this manuscript achieved its full potential, and for offering me wise and calming advice throughout this process. Thank you to Kenzi Sugihara, Nancy Sugihara and the entire team at SelectBooks for your enthusiasm for getting this material out to the world and your patience with my lack of publishing knowledge. I am indebted to my agent Bill Gladstone for recognizing the potential of this book and offering me safe passage into the world of publishing; thank you for saying "Yes" when it would have been so easy to turn me away.

Many friends and family members have been instrumental in providing me with encouragement along this path. To Deena Metzger, writing coach and spiritual guide: thank you for sending me off on my own journey of Living the Lessons and instilling in me the deep faith I needed in order to complete the task. Thanks also to spiritual teacher Rose Longhill for awakening my soul and reminding me of my purpose; your friendship and intuitive guidance have kept me on course through times of doubt and discouragement. For persistent optimism and an unshakable belief in me I thank my mother, Margaret Wyatt, whose powerful prayers sustain all that is good in the world. I am forever grateful to my beautiful children Aaron and Emily for offering me emotional support, thoughtful feedback, creative inspiration, and legal advice as I have taken on this new venture. It is my great fortune to be your mother, watching as you each make the world a better place every day. There are no sufficient words to express my gratitude to my husband, Larry, who willingly set out with me on this journey into the unknown. Thank you for building a beautiful sunroom as my writing studio, for supporting us financially through my career change, for the hours and hours you have spent patiently listening to my ideas and stories, for never losing faith in me, for keeping your sanity when I have been pushed to the edge of mine, for being my untiring advocate, and for selling my books, one at a time. My love for you has no beginning and no end as we travel together on this life path.

Finally, my gratitude extends beyond this life to those who have already departed our presence. I am thankful for my father whose life inspired me to work with dedication and persistence and whose death led me to become a hospice physician. This book would not exist without the hospice patients and their families who generously shared their stories with me and allowed me to participate in the final moments of their lives. I am forever grateful to them for teaching these spiritual lessons that have shaped my life and healed my own grief.

Introduction

"You know, you are going to have to live each of these lessons before you can write about them." This was the parting observation of my writing coach and spiritual mentor, Deena Metzger,[1] as I completed a weeklong workshop intended to jumpstart the creation of this book. I was puzzled at the time, wondering what she really meant, but I would soon begin to understand the truth and depth of her statement.

Shortly after that workshop my world changed drastically as my family and I moved to another state on short notice, requiring me to leave behind my beloved work with hospice. Although at that time I had already made considerable progress in dealing with grief over my father's suicide death, this sudden disruption in my life eventually plunged me back into deep despair, forcing me to revisit the pain of that loss. I was turned inside out as I delved once more into layers of old wounds and buried grief. As an unexpected result, I suddenly lost all inspiration and energy for writing this book; for months I was unable to write anything at all. Then, when the urge to put pen to paper rose to the surface again, I could write only about my father's death, which developed into my first book, *A Matter of Life & Death: Stories to Heal Loss & Grief.* After multiple failed attempts to begin writing about the seven lessons, I finally gave up, packing away all my notes and manuscripts in a cardboard box at the back of the closet. I immersed myself in my career and family, rarely thinking about the stories of the dying I had buried in that box.

Then, several years later, I met Rose Longhill,[2] a woman with psychic abilities who is also a spiritual master. After we became acquainted with one another, Rose confronted me with a revelation she had intuitively sensed: there was something important I was supposed to be doing with my life that I had been neglecting for a very long time. Instantly, my memory was flooded with the stories of my hospice patients and I knew I had to finish writing them. As I sat down to review the lessons once again, after so many years, I recognized that I had indeed lived all of them during that time. It was clear that I could now write this book, not just as an outside observer, but as a participant in the life-changing wisdom of *What Really Matters.*

Sources

The stories offered here are the true stories of actual patients I worked with as a hospice physician. Names have been changed, along with some non-essential details, to protect the identity of those patients and their families. I have matched each story with the particular lesson it best illustrates, though, ultimately, every lesson can be found in every story.

Where I have quoted verses from the New Testament, I have chosen to use as a source: *The Modern New Testament From the Aramaic*, translated by George Lamsa.[3] Aramaic is the language spoken by Jesus and his disciples and is rich with symbolism and meaning on many levels. While some verses may differ from the standard versions taken from Greek translations, I believe the Aramaic texts provide the deepest and most profound understanding of the message of Jesus.

Organization of this Book

In Part I, The Groundwork, I give the foundation for understanding the lessons to be learned from those who are nearing their death. In addition I explore the reasons why these lessons are important to master at this time in our existence.

In Part II, The Lessons, I have organized *What Really Matters* according to the seven statements attributed to Jesus as he was dying upon the cross, traditionally known as the Seven Last Words. Each chapter begins with a quote of the relative Word from one of the Gospels and a brief interpretation of its meaning. Over time I came to realize that the Seven Last Words reflected the same pattern I witnessed in the experiences of my patients. On further reflection, that made sense because Jesus was a man who was consciously facing His own imminent death. Through His dying words this master teacher of spiritual growth offers us a model to follow as we contemplate our own end of life.

Although I have used this aspect of the Christian tradition as a structure, the spiritual focus of these 7 Lessons is not limited to any particular religion or philosophy. In fact, these lessons represent universal truths that are common to all faiths and philosophical schools of thought. Even those who don't identify with any particular religious practice or spiritual tradition can benefit from these principles.

To further illustrate each of the lessons being taught, I've chosen a specific patient story to begin each chapter. These stories, filled with meaning and inspiration, are open to interpretation by the reader. I then present my analysis of The Seeds of wisdom that can be obtained from the story and The Fruits or character traits that can be manifested by learning the lesson of the story. This discussion details the work of spiritual growth that takes place in the garden of everyday life and includes additional brief stories to illustrate each point. The next section of each chapter, The View from the Garden, summarizes this day-to-day perspective of spiritual growth. Following that, the ultimate spiritual truth of each lesson is presented from the highest possible point of view, or The View from the Galaxy.

The last section of the book is Part III, The Harvest, which begins with "The Hollyhock Miracles," a story that presents the tale of my own spiritual growth through my work with two hospice patients over a two-year span of time. This story introduces the concept of "Living the Lessons" with patience, diligence and consistency and the ultimate blossoming of transformation that can result. The final chapter consists of a practical method for incorporating the 7 Lessons into daily life and offers guidance for beginning or continuing the process of spiritual development.

Purpose of this Book

My motivation for writing this book is twofold. First of all, after working in hospice for eight years of my medical career and sitting at the bedsides of hundreds of patients during their last moments of life, I developed within myself a calm and assured acceptance of death and the process of dying. I believe that it is worth sharing, especially since much of our society, and particularly our healthcare system, does not do enough to encourage meaningful conversations about the reality of dying or to allay some of the terror that accompanies this subject. It is my hope that those who read this book will experience newfound peace and comfort when they contemplate and make decisions for the end of their own lives, including an appreciation for hospice care.

Secondly, as I worked through each of these lessons personally, I began to recognize that they contain powerful spiritual truths that have helped transform every aspect of my life. As our world is currently in the midst of global crises threatening the environment, financial structures, and the safety and peace of all its inhabitants, the timing seems right for a renewed focus on such spiritual teachings. Because the resources of this planet are limited, we must be able to maximize our creativity and harness our productivity toward meaningful solutions to these threats; there is not a moment of time or an atom of energy to waste as we move into the future. The 7 lessons for living as taught by the stories of the dying in this book are designed to help us bring our own individual focus in harmony with the healing process that is needed throughout the world. While all of mankind must unite and center attention on crucial issues, each of us must learn in our own lifetimes what really matters. I pray that this book will provide a step in that direction.

Part I

✤

The Groundwork

Preparing for the Lessons

Ted, a hospice patient facing the last days of his life, turned to me with urgency to say, "I've only just learned what really matters in life now that I am at the time of my death. Why didn't I know this earlier? You've got to tell other people to pay attention NOW and learn these lessons before it is too late."

*　　*　　*

And in this way the seed for this book was planted many years ago at the bedside of a dying man. Over the next few years as I participated in the final days of many other hospice patients I began to recognize that there is a profound opportunity at the end of life for transformation to occur, bringing with it a new and wise perspective of the meaning and purpose of life. In addition, I witnessed the manifestation of beauty and peace that accompanied the last moments of life, alleviating much of my own fear of death. As a calm observer of the end of life and the lessons it provides, I began to experience transformation and spiritual growth within myself, ultimately finding hope rather than dread in the prospect of dying. These lessons I learned became for me the central framework of my life, informing my decisions and guiding my actions toward those things that make a difference in this world, toward what really matters.

Why This Book Matters

As we enter the second decade of the 21st century, uneasiness abounds and a sense of doom is prevalent everywhere we turn. Scholars, philosophers, seers, sages, and prophets all tell us that our planet is on the verge of some sort of cataclysmic global shift, predicted to occur within the next ten years. No one knows how this turning point will unfold or what impact this shift will have upon each of us, but it is likely to be a profound transition, sending ripples of volatility across the entire world.

Meanwhile, global disturbances, such as acts of terrorism, natural disasters, military hostilities, the world economic crisis, climate change, and even the political unrest in the Middle East, are all harbingers of the changes to come. Throughout history a pattern has developed that the "old" established and stable structures, whether they are societies, cities, cultures, beliefs, buildings, or forests, must break down in order to allow the growth of something new. In a similar manner, the destructive processes that seem to be taking hold all around us are actually preparing the way for future transformations.

However, our American society has been caught in a selfish and materialistic phase of development for several decades, as evidenced by the "me generation" of the 1980s and the rapid rise of consumerism since that time. As a result, many of us are not equipped to cope with sudden disruption and disintegration in our world. We have neglected to develop the emotional and spiritual tools that will be required in order to rise above crisis and continue to thrive. This fact has been evident during the recent global economic downturn, as in a recent U.S. national survey on drug use and mental health services one in ten adults reported having been prescribed a mental health medication in the past year.[4] In addition, the most frequently prescribed medication in the country is now Vicodin, a narcotic pain-reliever.[5] It appears that the pain of our everyday lives is causing us to turn to pharmaceutical agents for relief because we lack the internal resources to cope with our struggles. If this current economic situation is just a foreshadowing of a future crisis, how are we going to survive when there is far more suffering at hand?

The hoped-for role of this book is that it provides a framework through which to view the coming shift as well as a crash course in the spiritual skills necessary to navigate disaster. It is time now to turn our energy and attention away from the self-absorbed pursuits of the past toward a goal of awakening and maturing as conscious beings. The lessons presented here form a foundation from which spiritual growth can occur. While these teachings represent ancient and timeless wisdom, the urgency behind the message is contemporary and unique to our current situation. We stand upon a precipice between dissolution and transcendence. Do not underestimate the fact that our next steps have the potential to determine the course of the future.

The Dying as Teachers

After my father's death I was left floundering, having lost my belief that this world is a safe place in which to exist. While I desperately searched for answers, I was able to find solace and guidance in the stories of the dying patients I cared for in my work with hospice. These patients and their families shared with me not only the intimate details of their final days, but also the collective wisdom they had gathered throughout this lifetime. In some cases, patients attained phenomenal insight and clarity in their spiritual vision during the crisis of dying and were eager to share this knowledge. For others, the transformation was evident in their behavior or appearance rather than conveyed through their words. And at times the caregivers of the patient experienced profound evolution as they participated in their loved one's last moments. In every case these stories of how we live and die on this planet are inspirational, poignant, and uplifting. On many occasions the patients themselves asked me to tell their stories, regretting that they would not have enough time to share their newly recognized wisdom with others. I have carried their histories with me, awaiting this opportunity to fulfill my promise to them at last. Therefore, this book is a tribute to those patients who so generously taught me the lessons of life and death.

It is important to understand why we, who are very much alive right now, have anything to learn from those who have already faced their mortality and passed on from this existence. As will be shown, these hospice stories come from individuals who died from chronic, terminal illnesses and spent a great deal of time anticipating and confronting their own death. They lived within a state of crisis for prolonged periods, learning all the while how to cope with tragedy and continue to find meaning in every remaining day. As we look ahead to uncertain times and potential threats to the comforts of life as we know it, we can benefit from the wisdom of those who have already negotiated a dangerous passage and who desperately wanted us to grasp the knowledge they had finally attained. We honor them by learning from their histories and using their lessons to magnify our own spiritual growth in preparation for what lies ahead. It is time to gather our courage and face our own mortality.

Denial of Death

There is no place on Earth we can look without seeing death. In the transition from one season to the next, in the tangle of the spider's web, in the falling of a star across the night sky—we behold the Truth of Life: that matter disintegrates, that life dies. Our mortality is the one most fundamental characteristic we share with every life form on earth—from plankton to platypus, from amoeba to aspen grove—all will die. Considering the abundant evidence that exists all around us, it is an unequivocal certainty that our current lives are going to come to an end. And yet, it seems that our modern society has forgotten this fundamental truth of human existence: death is unavoidable.

At the beginning of the last century most people died at home. They were tended to in their final days by family members who also prepared their bodies for burial, perhaps "laying them out" on the kitchen table where they were bathed and dressed one last time.[6] Death was a constant presence in daily life then, resulting often from infections and injuries for which there were few effective treatments. Even children were exposed to the normality of death from an early age. But following the rise of modern medicine, with advancing technology and miraculous, life-saving drugs such as penicillin, death became an outcome that seemed to be temporarily avoidable. We began to feel some confidence in our ability to fend off the "grim reaper" and concurrently began to lose awareness of the connection of death to life. As a consequence, we have forgotten the truth that our earthly mortality ultimately gives meaning and value to our physical life on this planet. To our detriment, the fear of death has consumed us and led us to expend increasing effort and healthcare dollars toward preserving life at all costs. For example, approximately 25% of the annual Medicare budget is spent on aggressive, life-sustaining care during the final month of life, much of which is futile and may actually prolong suffering rather than enhance life.[7]

The Gift of Mortality

As we delve further into the study of life and death, acceptance of a fundamental belief will help us interpret and prioritize the lessons being presented here. This belief holds that our life on this planet is a spiritual journey taking place in a physical realm. In other words, we exist as physical beings precisely for the purpose of learning certain spiritual truths during our time on Earth. There is no question that our human bodies are sublime vehicles for gathering information and absorbing the wisdom of life with five senses to experience the diversity of nature manifested through smells, sounds, sights, tastes, and textures; with multifunctional limbs to allow us to move and take action; with various organs to help us encounter pleasure and take in sustenance; with neurological linkages for acquiring knowledge, dreaming, and reasoning; and with built-in systems for growth, repair, and healing. What an amazing gift is this physical existence we have inherited. Yet life is a gift that will not last. These bodies of ours are destined to fade and wear down as we proceed through time, using up the physical learning potential that was bestowed upon us at birth.

Then, in the latter days of life, a gradual shift in focus must occur, away from the pursuits of the physical world toward the truths of the spiritual realm.[8] As we lose certain functions and capacities on the physical level, we have an opportunity to gain even more intangible wisdom and understanding. In fact, the soul shines through ever more brightly as the physical body fades. Many times during my home visits with the dying, I observed a beautiful, soft light surrounding the patient in their bed. I would first look around for a hidden lamp or some other source of the illumination until I realized that I was seeing the light of the soul, unobscured by the physical body, which was rapidly dissolving away. From this perspective it is perfect that we are mortal beings. For if we could maintain youthful, strong bodies forever, no shift of attention toward the spiritual would be likely to occur. We might stay permanently stalled at the materialistic, egocentric level of development with no impetus to move ahead.

No Time to Waste

However, we might argue, if we can anticipate learning these lessons at the end of life, why bother to study them now? Why not wait until our final moments to focus in on the spiritual aspect of existence? The answer is that the rate of change in every area of life is accelerating as we speak. Technology is advancing faster than most of us can keep pace and so, too, are the challenges we face on this planet. In order to be prepared for the transitions of the future we must master certain spiritual tasks now. We cannot delay the necessary steps of our growth any longer.

In fact, as the dying patients themselves recognized, these lessons should be learned earlier in our existence so that they can be utilized for the good of all life. Again, as we stand upon this precipice between transcendence and dissolution, there is no time to waste.

Another obvious reason to learn the lessons from the dying now is that there are no guarantees in this life. Not one of us knows when or how we might depart this existence and we have no assurance that we will be granted a slow course toward death during our elder years. We would each be wise to make the most of every learning opportunity now since we do not know if it will become available to us again in the future.

The View from the Garden

The process of spiritual growth can be compared to raising a garden: planting seeds and harvesting the crops that result. Imagine that you were given at birth a small patch of land and a few seeds. You have no control over the location of your garden plot, whether it is in a fertile valley or on a rocky mountainside, and you are unable to change the quality of the soil it contains. Also, you cannot determine the amount of sun, rain, wind, or hail that falls upon your garden. But you are responsible for planting the seeds you have been given, seeking additional seeds to grow, nurturing and tending what you have planted, and bringing in the harvest when it is ready. According to this metaphor some aspects of your existence in this life are out of your control: your birthplace, family members, culture and society, and your inherited qualities and assets. But you do have a responsibility to utilize the factors that *can* be altered, such as your effort and intentions, to create the best possible life from the raw material presented to you at your birth. This is the essence of spiritual growth: to employ all that has been given in this life (including both the positive and the negative factors), manifest the greatest potential available, and recognize that everything, including the Self, is sacred.

In keeping with this metaphor of the garden, the Lessons for living from the stories of the dying can supply you with additional seeds to sow in your own plot of land so that you might one day harvest the fruits they provide. Perhaps it is too soon for some of these seeds to grow right now, but they can always blossom at a later time when the conditions are favorable. Just hold on to them until you know that you are ready to begin cultivating the lessons and being transformed by the truths they contain. But don't forget that toiling in the garden—that is, working on your spiritual growth—is actually the only reason you are here, the only thing that really matters in this lifetime.

THE VIEW FROM THE GALAXY

The metaphor of a garden requiring constant attention and care is a helpful way to think about the day-to-day events of your life and the work that is necessary in order to grow spiritually. The garden represents the "small picture" view of life that informs most of your actions and decisions every day. However, there is another perspective that you should try to develop, as well. This is the "big picture" view of human existence which requires you to look beyond your own individual concerns to recognize that there is something greater going on in this life, something that encompasses the entire planet and all of mankind. You can achieve this perspective by taking a step back from the small details and trying to see the complete panorama of existence, as if you were looking down from a point high above the Earth.

Astronauts have described the moment they caught sight of Earth through the small porthole window of their spaceship as filled with wonder—a sudden realization of a higher purpose, of what really matters. Edgar Mitchell, who walked on the moon during the Apollo 14 space mission, wrote about seeing the Earth become visible from behind the rim of the moon as "a sparkling blue and white jewel, a light, delicate sky-blue sphere laced with slowly swirling veils of white, rising gradually like a small pearl in a thick sea of black mystery." Mitchell went on to describe the epiphany that occurred for him at that moment: "The presence of divinity became almost palpable, and I knew that life in the universe was not just an accident based on random processes ... the knowledge came to me directly." The power of this vision so deeply inspired Mitchell that after retiring from the space program he founded the Institute of Noetic Sciences, dedicated to advancing the science of consciousness in order to promote transformation.

But this amazing and enlightening view from above is not just available to space travelers who have escaped the Earth's gravity. A hospice patient once described to me a very similar vision that came to him one night in a dream.

*   *   *

Eugene was in his seventies and close to death from severe heart disease that had affected him for most of his adult life. His first heart attack had occurred thirty years earlier and caused extensive damage to his heart muscle. He and his wife Beth had been told then that his lifespan might be shortened because his cardiac function was so critically compromised. And so, the couple had prepared themselves for this possible future. They talked at length about what life might be like for Beth as a widow and planned ahead financially so that she would have some security when that day came. Over the next fifteen years, Beth made herself ready to face her old age alone while Eugene worked to make peace with his past.

But then, an unexpected tragedy struck. Beth died suddenly at home of a ruptured aneurysm in her brain. Eugene held her in his arms, awaiting the arrival of an ambulance, as she slipped away from him. He was devastated and totally bewildered by this development. Beth was not the one who was supposed to die young! She had always been totally healthy—there had never been a reason for them to prepare for HER death. He felt bitter and betrayed by God and life itself as he sank into depression. All of his preparatory work had been in anticipation of his own death; he had no idea how to go on living alone without his beloved wife. For the next twelve years Eugene floundered in despair and depression, hating every moment of his life and listing in his mind all of the joys that had been denied to Beth by her untimely death. "It's not fair!" became his mantra, repeated angrily over and over again to everyone he knew.

But just a few days before I first met Eugene, everything changed for him because of a dream. He described that in the dream he had been transported through space to a star far away in the galaxy. From there he was able to look down at the Earth and see all the details of his and Beth's lives as they had unfolded. At once, from that lofty perspective, Eugene recognized that somehow everything had been perfect, just as it had occurred. He saw that there was a purpose and a plan for each event that had taken place, including Beth's death from the aneurysm. With light sparkling in his eyes and an angelic smile on his face, Eugene said to me, "We think that life is unfair to us, but that's just because we can only see it from the Earth. If we could always see what life looks like from up above we would know that it's ALL fair! I know this is true: Everything that happens to us is fair in God's eyes. We just don't understand how it all works."

Eugene would live out the next few months in peace and contentment, once again preparing to leave this life. Free of the bitterness that had haunted him for twelve years, he talked to everyone he saw about his revelation, explaining to the best of his ability the true meaning of fairness and the power of changing one's point of view.

*   *   *

Multiple Perspectives

From Eugene's story we can see that our interpretation of life and its occurrences can change depending on how we look at it. The view from the perspective of one individual life tends to focus on details and be tossed by emotional ups and downs, just like the storms that play havoc with our planted crops. The concerns and wellbeing of that one person take priority at this "garden" level. Thus, Eugene could see the death of his wife only as senseless and unfair when he looked at it from the small perspective of his tiny garden. However, when he was shown a bigger view he recognized that all the individual aspects of life, whether they seemed "good" or "bad" to him actually fit together in a perfect pattern. When we are able to step back and look at life from the "big picture" vantage point of the galaxy, we can see that there are actually no individual concerns that are not part of the whole of life. Everything is connected and everything is one. This view provides a sense of calmness and equanimity toward the challenges of life, almost turning our attitudes upside down. What seems to be unfair is really fair, what hurts us actually helps us, what we cling to is not what really matters.

The process of growing spiritually, of becoming more fully conscious and aware, consists of being able to view life from the galaxy even while you toil in the garden. You must be able to put all your effort into the day-to-day tasks of planting, cultivating, and harvesting in your garden while simultaneously holding in your awareness the fact that from a higher perspective the details of the soil, the seeds, and even the crops you yield, are not really important. It is your awareness—your ability to take the highest possible perspective toward everything—that really matters. This sounds confusing and paradoxical and it is—which is why it takes a lifetime to truly grasp the nature of spiritual growth.

However, you need only to remember this: the process begins with your own garden and the seeds to be sown from the Lessons from the dying. Start wherever you are and trust that growth will come, as surely as each tiny blade of grass thrusts itself through the soil every spring.

The Dance of Life

"Let your life lightly dance
on the edges of time
like dew on the tip of a leaf."

-Rabindranath Tagore

If you spend time observing a flower garden you will quickly recognize the continual dance of life that is unfolding there. A shimmering drop of dew falls upon a leaf, setting the entire stem in delicate motion; a faintly whispered breeze stirs brightly colored blossoms into an elegant waltz; a tiny ladybug flies away leaving a trembling petal in its wake. The components necessary for this dance to occur are the same elements that emerge over and over again in the 7 Lessons learned from the dying: timing, balance, rhythm, and grace. Timing refers to the clock of infinity where change requires a lifetime of work, but transformation occurs in an instant. Balance is the equal joining of two seemingly opposite forces that enable one another to survive. Rhythm is the flow of life and energy that permeates everything around us. Grace is the generosity of abundance, like the garden that freely bestows its blossoms and fruits upon us. As you read these lessons, keep in mind the perpetual dance that moves throughout each story; the significance of timing, balance, rhythm, and grace as they each unfold; and the two partners, Life and Death, holding one another closely, swaying eternally to the music of the Universe.

Part II

❧

The Lessons

LESSON 1

Suffering: EMBRACE YOUR DIFFICULTIES

"I thirst."

-John 19:28

The first lesson taught to us by the dying is "Embrace Your Difficulties" and deals with our approach to Suffering. In many ways, this is the most difficult of the lessons for us to learn, but it forms the foundation for all other teachings and is therefore presented in the beginning. When we study the remaining lessons, our perspective of suffering will deepen and broaden as we begin to awaken and recognize that our difficulties in life open the door to our transformation.

When Jesus was dying on the cross, His only reference to physical suffering consisted of just two words, "I thirst." In the Aramaic language spoken by Jesus, the word *tzheyn* can be translated not only as "thirst," but can also mean "dried out or parched inwardly." This broader interpretation of the word includes both the physical condition of dryness and a sense of spiritual and emotional longing. In addition, the use of the word *tzheyn* implies being dried out intentionally, for a greater purpose, as when a gourd is hollowed out and dried to form a container for water.[9]

We understand that Jesus suffered intensely during the process of His dying, yet He accepted it courageously, embracing the pain without bitterness or complaint. He knew that His anguish and death were necessary and would bring about a greater good for all of mankind. This is the attitude we are asked to embody as we face the burdens and tragedies that come to us in life: embrace the difficulties, face them head-on with courage and equanimity, and create something beautiful from the ruins. The following is the story of Ruby, who managed to live this lesson well.

THE VISION OF AN ARTIST

In spite of suffering from severe heart disease that resulted in constant fatigue, Ruby was a vibrant and vivacious woman at the age of eighty-one. Her face, lined with wrinkles, was soft and glowing while her eyes sparkled with joy even though she was legally blind. Ruby had lost her vision gradually over the past fifteen years due to macular degeneration, a condition that may have been caused by the same extremely high blood pressure levels that had affected her heart. Ruby was now approaching the end of her life with a heart that was barely able to function due to the damage sustained over the years. But she was eager to tell me her story as she arranged a place for me to sit at her bedside.

She told me her husband had died at a young age, leaving her with three children to raise alone. She had worked hard for many years to support herself and her family, making numerous sacrifices along the way. Finally in her mid-fifties, when her children were all on their own, she had time to explore her own interests and discovered that she possessed great artistic talent that had never before been recognized. Ruby learned how to use a weaving loom during these years and created beautiful tapestries from watercolor designs she had painted herself.

Within a few years, however, Ruby began to notice some problems with her vision. She ignored it until she started having difficulty seeing the tiny warp and weft threads in her weaving loom. When she consulted an eye doctor she learned of her condition and the fact that it would likely grow worse over time. While there are now treatments available to slow down the progression of macular degeneration, nothing existed at that time to help her. She was told that her vision would continue to gradually deteriorate.

Ruby was forced to give up her weaving shortly after this because she couldn't see well enough to create the intricate designs she had perfected. She felt despair for some time, wondering how she would fill her hours and utilize the creativity that brimmed within her. Then she read that a class in woodcarving was being offered at a local junior college. She signed up and quickly fell in love with the art of carving. Using small hand knives, Ruby whittled complicated patterns into rectangular blocks of aspen, butternut, and basswood. Because she could hold the wood close to her eyes while she worked, her poor vision did not interfere with her craftsmanship. Her teacher remarked that he had never had a student learn so rapidly or demonstrate such talent for carving. While her watercolor paintings and woven tapestries had been beautiful, Ruby felt then that she had actually found her true calling in woodcarving. Her pieces were indeed remarkable works of art and surpassed in quality even those created by her teacher.

For the next five years or so, Ruby flourished with her artistry to produce brilliant hand-carved figures and relief designs, almost forgetting about the progressive condition that was affecting her sight. But then a sudden change occurred. Practically overnight Ruby lost her remaining vision. She had been so absorbed in her creative work that she had not really prepared herself for this decline. Everything in her life changed in an instant as she became dependent on her children for help and unable to express her creativity.

For a while Ruby sank into hopelessness and lost her will to live. If she could no longer produce art, which she believed was the true purpose of her life, then perhaps there was no reason for her existence. The blackness of the world perceived by her eyes was echoed by the black despair she felt within. But one day she received a visit from her woodcarving teacher who had become a friend through the years. Understanding the depth of Ruby's pain over losing her creative outlet, he had consulted the ceramics department at his school and obtained a gift for Ruby. Opening her hands, he placed in them a lump of smooth, cool modeling clay, moist and ready to form. With his encouragement Ruby began to knead the substance with her fingers, enjoying the feel of the supple and responsive clay. The teacher told Ruby he would return for another visit in two weeks and left her still holding the solid block of clay.

Several days passed before Ruby felt the energy to touch the clay again. But when she picked it up this time, a familiar spark of creative inspiration passed through her. She began to work on the clay, her fingers moving swiftly and knowingly as if she had been doing this all her life. Though she could not see the shape her hands were molding Ruby could picture in her mind the form she was creating. She divided the clay and crafted three different structures over the next few days. When her teacher finally returned, Ruby waved her hand toward the shelf where her unfired clay pieces had been left to dry. Waiting nervously for his critique, she heard him gasp as he looked at her work. Finally he spoke, telling her that while her wood-carving had been the finest he had ever seen from a student, her clay sculptures were so magnificent they made the wooden figures seem ordinary. He was truly amazed, having expected only to provide Ruby with a means of passing the time, never anticipating that she would discover even greater artistic talent within.

Ruby continued to mold her unseen masterpieces in clay until she died. She told me during our first meeting that she believed she had to lose her external eyesight in order to release her internal vision. When she could no longer see what was outside of her, she was finally free to look within and manifest all the beauty that was waiting there. Though it is difficult for others to understand, Ruby considered the loss of her eyesight the greatest gift of her life. She was certain that she would not have discovered her full potential without the blindness that led to her perfect inner vision. Ruby's ability to embrace everything on her path—her talents as well as her weaknesses, and her adversities as well as her good fortune—led to a fulfilled life and a peaceful passing away. Indeed, Ruby had managed to create not only watercolors, tapestries, woodcarvings, and clay sculptures that were works of art, but a life that was a masterpiece as well.

THE SEEDS OF SUFFERING

Ruby's story teaches us that suffering, when fully embraced, can lead to finding a higher purpose and creating a fulfilled life. In order to understand this process, there are several qualities or "seeds" of suffering to be studied and mastered.

Suffering is Universal

Everywhere you look on this planet some type of suffering exists. Animals in the wild must hunt for food everyday and are preyed upon by larger animals. Forests are razed by clear-cutting or wiped out by tiny insects such as the pine bark beetle, and plants compete with one another for space and nutrients only to be trampled underfoot by an unsuspecting hiker. Watch just a few moments of the nightly news and you will be overwhelmed by the magnitude of human suffering that occurs for people from all walks of life across the globe. This experience of suffering is one of the characteristics that unites mankind with all of nature. Every living thing suffers and every living thing dies.

Yet at times, in our narrow vision, we see only our own individual suffering, losing sight of the rest of the world. In our anguish we forget that pain connects us with every creature on the planet, that suffering is a common bond shared by all of life. If we could view our own agony as part of the spectrum of all suffering, endured by all people throughout the ages, then somehow our individual circumstances might seem less oppressive. We are not alone in our torment. We belong to an enormous community with vast experience in the area of suffering and we have access to great wisdom to help us on our journey.

The Buddhist tradition teaches a story about an Indian woman named Kisha-Gotami that illustrates the universality of suffering. The mother of a beautiful young child, Kisha-Gotami had lost her husband in a tragic accident. Her pain over his death had been severe, but love for her child had helped her cope and survive. Then, one horrible day she awoke to find that her baby had died as well. Nearly mad with grief, she carried the lifeless body of her child to a mountainside where the Buddha was teaching his followers. Kisha-Gotami begged him to alleviate her pain by bringing her baby back to life. With great compassion, Buddha agreed to perform that miracle for her if she would bring him some mustard seeds from a village household where no one had ever died. Kisha-Gotami rushed from house to house, begging for mustard seeds to bring her child back to life. But she was unable to find a single home where no one had ever died. Eventually she returned to the feet of the Buddha and wept, finally understanding that her suffering, though intense, connected her with every other person in the village. Surrounded by this support, Kisha-Gotami was finally able to let go of her grief and heal her pain.

As this story illustrates, when shared with all of mankind, our losses can be easier to tolerate. But if we see ourselves as separate and isolated the burden is ours alone to bear and we have only our own strength to call upon. Sharing the weight of suffering requires us to face our own pain head-on and acknowledge that it is a part of every life, leaving no room for denial or repression.

Though the evidence is ample that suffering is universal, suffering is still feared and reviled in our Western culture. Much of our costly system of healthcare is devoted to the relief of physical suffering while often ignoring the presence of emotional and spiritual pain. When we seek to eliminate suffering at all costs without understanding its purpose and meaning, we frequently end up worsening the very misery we sought to alleviate. Ultimately, none of us can avoid suffering during our lifetimes; and it is how we manage to cope with our difficulties that will determine the quality of the life we live. This is a truth that becomes totally clear to the dying and that we must learn, as well.

Suffering is Necessary

"Losses are a part of life—universal, unavoidable, inexorable.
And these losses are necessary because we grow
by losing and leaving and letting go."

-Judith Viorst

The next, and perhaps most difficult concept for us to understand, is that suffering is a *necessary* part of life. In our own human growth and development each new stage we achieve requires us to give up something from the previous stage, enduring loss as we struggle to move forward and master new skills. The toddler gives up crawling and accepts the pain and frustration of repeated falls in order to learn to walk, and the teenager gives up the security of home and accepts the risk of rejection in order to find an individual identity in the world. Each new accomplishment requires the loss of something previously cherished. Furthermore, without these losses and the suffering they entail there would be no growth, no progress in this human life. As we have already seen, in all of nature and human existence, suffering and death are essential in order to break down the old and make way for the new. In fact, the natural world offers many beautiful illustrations of the necessity of suffering, which can help us to grasp this difficult concept.

As one example, in the natural life cycle of a wetland area occasional drought is required for rejuvenation of the life forms in the swamp. While many water-borne plants and animals die when the drought occurs, the drying out of the swamp bed allows oxygen to return to the soil.

This, in turn, leads to an increase in the rate of decomposition of the dead plants, which releases nutrients back into the soil, allowing seeds that have been dormant for long periods to germinate and grow. Without drought the wetlands area would stop thriving and become stagnant. So the health of the entire marsh ecosystem depends on the stress of drought that comes along every few years.

In another example, the jack pine tree produces a cone that is tightly closed with seeds sealed inside underneath its compact scales. The only thing that causes the scales to open and release the seeds is intense heat, such as that produced by a forest fire. So a new jack pine tree can only grow from those seeds in the aftermath of a fire. Clearly, in this case, destruction, or suffering, is necessary for new growth to occur. And in addition, destruction itself actually brings with it the seeds of hope, of new life. From this perspective, when suffering comes it contains within it the potential for transformation even though we may not recognize it. In other words, the transformative process is "unlocked" by the act of suffering and often cannot occur without the experience of suffering.

One of the reasons why suffering is necessary for human beings is that we identify so thoroughly with the physical and mental aspects of our existence, keeping our spiritual nature tightly closed inside, like the seeds of the jack pine tree. Our egos delight in the abilities of the physical body and believe that the body is everything that matters. For many of us this dependence on the physical must be gradually broken down by aging or illness, so that attention can be shifted to spiritual matters. In fact, physical suffering can be a threshold or doorway to greater awareness, to spiritual growth.

Many indigenous cultures have used painful rituals as part of the ceremony of initiation to adulthood or spiritual enlightenment, such as the Sun Dance practiced by the Plains Indians of North America. While our society may view these ceremonies as barbaric, their native wisdom demonstrates that suffering is not to be avoided or feared, but to be sought after and welcomed. In addition, many religious groups have historically practiced intentional suffering, such as fasting, sitting in prayer or meditation for long periods of time, crawling great distances on hands and knees, fire walking, or lying on a bed of nails. Once again, in these instances suffering is valued and revered because it calls forth the Spirit and permits opportunities for growth.

Suffering is Unique

While it is true that every human must suffer, it is also true that it is a unique experience for each individual. Some must endure intense physical pain as part of the process of disease or injury, while for others the emotional pain of loss is the most severe, causing depression and anxiety. In addition, suffering can occur on a spiritual level when it is caused by a separation from or lack of awareness of the soul. Some dying patients hold on to intense spiritual anger, blaming God for the outcome of their lives and must struggle to find peace in their final days. When emotional and spiritual discomforts are present they can intensify the experience of physical pain, making it much more difficult to treat physical discomfort with conventional methods. In such cases, in addition to the use of pain relievers, it is crucial that the emotional and spiritual issues be addressed. Medications alone will not be successful in alleviating this type of pain. Even for those of us who are not at the end of life this fact is important: physical symptoms will be worsened by unaddressed emotional and spiritual pain. Effective treatment for any condition requires looking at suffering from every point of view and at every level. Each person must be treated as an individual with a distinctive history and a quality of suffering that is totally unique.

Finally, each of us will suffer during our time on Earth, and no man's suffering should be judged as greater or less than that of another. Our suffering is given to us in service of our spiritual growth and therefore is perfect for us. We cannot judge the extent of the suffering of anyone else and should have equal compassion for everyone, even those who appear to have an easier life. Much suffering lies hidden inside and is not visible to those who can see only what is on the outside.

THE FRUITS OF SUFFERING

When we are able to embrace our suffering and face it willingly, there are several benefits we will receive to help us live a more fulfilled life. These "fruits," like the actual fruit we harvest from the seeds we plant, have in common the fact that they require time in order to grow. In our society time is a precious commodity and most of us are feeling a shortage of it as we multi-task our way through our responsibilities. Not only do we resent giving up time for things that are not on our agenda but we also tend to shortchange the people and activities that are important to us. Suffering, however, has its own timeframe, slowing down and prolonging each moment. And during times of difficulty when we do manage to slow the day-to-day pace to breathe in deeply the oxygen of life and contemplate the experience of our suffering, we can learn valuable lessons that cannot be so effectively taught by any other situation.

Humility

One of the fruits of suffering is the ability to be humble, to behave without excessive pride. Humility is a character trait that is rare to find in our modern-day society. Accustomed to having things go their way, many people conduct themselves, both in private and public, with an attitude of arrogance and entitlement. Just observe people in line at the grocery store or bank and you will see examples of rudeness, impatience, and irritation because this activity is not proceeding according to their schedule. Our politicians, sports figures, and entertainers, who are frequently in the public eye as role models, often display self-important, egotistical behavior in their social interactions. And in everyday situations, people in general are becoming more selfish and more uncivil in their treatment of others, thinking only of their own needs and concerns. The rapid pace and stress of our daily life seems to contribute to this condition because behaving with humility requires some time-consuming thought and focus.

However, suffering has the ability to strip away your self-importance and bring your ego down to ground level. From this vantage point you will experience an increased awareness of the needs of others and concern for the welfare of the whole. The myth of invincibility and superiority is destroyed by suffering, leading you to a sense of gratitude and appreciation for the fragility of life. Without the drive to perform and produce you will have more time for simple acts and quiet pursuits. When the mind is not full of egocentric thoughts, you will find room to notice others and behave with intentional kindness, a hallmark of humility.

Patience

An increased ability to withstand difficulties and tolerate adversity is another fruit of suffering. As day to-day life has become more leisurely and we no longer have to struggle just to survive, we have lost some of our capacity to bear up under hardship and allow the passage of time required for the situations of life to resolve. People everywhere are looking for quick fixes and instant solutions to their problems, rushing into the future with no respect for the timing of life.

But suffering can linger for many months or even years, often without the smallest glimpse of improvement. In order for you to survive this degree of suffering you must learn how to endure, to tolerate pain without giving up. Once your capacity for patience is increased, you can face other situations in life with confidence and fearlessness, knowing that you are a survivor and have learned to overcome obstacles.

Resilience

Resilience is one of the character traits demonstrated by Ruby as she coped with her progressive loss of eyesight. Bouncing back after each setback, Ruby went on to accomplish even greater things rather than being defeated by her blindness. When you "practice" at managing your suffering with humility and learn to endure for as long as it takes, you will begin to live with a certain flexibility and spontaneity, recovering more quickly from difficulties and with less overall damage. This attribute will benefit your life in every possible way. It will help you to move out into the world and face even larger challenges, knowing you have the capacity to bear any suffering they entail. Being a leader and problem-solver in our society requires resilience and it cannot be attained without the lessons taught by suffering.

Connectedness

As Kisha-Gotami learned, suffering is the common denominator shared by all people. When you are able to embrace this fact you begin to rise above your own difficulties and see beyond them to the needs of all mankind. This sense of connectedness can provide you with comfort, but also lead you to reach out to others and help them in their distress. There is no greater antidote to suffering than assisting someone else who is in pain. Because we are all connected to one another, when you help someone else you end up finding the way through your own struggles. This is one reason why hospice work is so fulfilling for the healthcare providers who pursue this field: they find that their own suffering diminishes when being of service to their fellow man.

THE VIEW FROM THE GARDEN

No matter where life takes you, suffering will come to you in one form or another. While your suffering is unique to you, it does not set you apart from the rest of creation; rather, it connects you with all living things. Difficulties are a normal and ordinary aspect of the unfolding of life. Attempting to run away or hide from your distress will only increase your pain in the future, so face your problems head-on. Give up searching for a logical explanation for your suffering or someone to blame for your discomfort. Those activities serve only to distract you from the work of embracing your difficulties. Be humble and patient as you learn to cope with the struggles of existence. Resist any temptation to use your suffering to manipulate others or gain power over them. Instead, use your pain to open the door to your own transformation as you examine the remaining lessons from the dying.

THE VIEW FROM THE GALAXY

Take a journey now to a distant star in the galaxy or to a spaceship returning from exploring the vast reaches of the Universe. Look down upon our planet and the life forms that flourish here. From this vantage point you can see that suffering is ultimately a gift, a divine assistance for your spiritual growth. Life, throughout your time on this planet, presents you with the suffering you need in order to grow in awareness and manifest the full potential you have within. Suffering takes you down to the core of your being—demolishing illusions and fantasies in the process—to a place of pure honesty, pure pain and, ultimately, pure joy. You cannot reach the heights of spiritual awareness without descending first to the depths of your suffering. Practices that seek only to eliminate suffering, including Western medicine, are slightly misguided. You must first embrace and embody suffering, making it your own, in order to transform and transcend suffering. It is your creative transformation brought about by suffering that brings value to your living. Part of the challenge for you during this lifetime is to enter the portal of suffering in order to complete your spiritual growth. There is no other purpose for your suffering or even for your existence. Rise to the occasion and accept the gift that has been given to you, no matter what form it takes.

*   *   *

Alice was a cancer patient who, from the beginning, was able to find meaning in her suffering. When an advanced osteosarcoma was found in her femur she refused an amputation that might have alleviated some of her pain, but would not have altered the course of her disease. Alice said to me, "I expect to have pain. Pain is just part of the process when you have cancer." Then, with a look of both determination and calmness in her eyes, she added, "I intend to experience everything life has to offer before I die, including pain." Her willingness to open to suffering, even to embrace it, enabled Alice to tolerate the physical pain she was asked to bear. She was never angry or frightened or inconsolable throughout her dying process—she simply observed what was happening to her body with interest and courage. Her spiritual foundation was strong. She recognized a wisdom and meaning within her suffering and met it with both grace and gratitude.

*   *   *

Dostoevski wrote, "There is only one thing that I dread: not to be worthy of my sufferings." The way to be worthy of the gift of suffering is to keep moving through it, on a path that traverses the remaining six lessons. If you cannot now see the blessing, the gift, in your suffering, hold on and keep working at it, for it will be revealed to you one day. When you have completed the journey of the 7 Lessons, you will be able to look back with new sight and recognize the importance of suffering in your life. From this vantage point, you can stop labeling events in your life as either "bad" or "good." See the possibility in everything to lead to growth and fulfillment.

WHAT REALLY MATTERS ABOUT SUFFERING

Suffering opens the doorway to spiritual growth.
Embrace your difficulties with equanimity,
recognizing that they are a gift.

LESSON 2

Love: LET YOUR HEART BE BROKEN

"Woman behold your son; behold your mother."
-John 19:26,27

When we have plummeted to the depth of our suffering and faced it openly and honestly, we must then begin to learn the next lesson from the dying: "Let Your Heart Be Broken," which is the challenge to experience true Love. When we truly love another, that act results in the opening of our hearts so that we can achieve greater depth, compassion and growth. However, much of the sentiment that is labeled *"love"* in our society is really self-seeking, superficial emotion that strives only to make us feel good. True love actually hurts and can rip us to pieces. And that, we must come to realize, is the beautiful gift of true love.

When Jesus was dying on the cross, He spoke the words above to his mother Mary and to His "beloved disciple" whom many believe was John. As the oldest son of Mary, Jesus bore the traditional responsibility to ensure that His mother was cared for until the end of her life. Even while He was completing His own agonizing, final moments of existence and fulfilling His spiritual destiny, His love for His mother superseded everything else in that point of time. In the last act of His breaking human heart, Jesus commended His dear mother to the care of His best friend, cutting His earthly ties to them so that He could transcend and form a heavenly bond instead.

Thus, the nature of true love, as we shall learn, is not to elevate us to the clouds where we hear beautiful music and dwell in blissful oblivion, but to break us open and expose our shadow, allowing genuine healing to begin. The heart must be broken to reveal the light of compassion and to hold all the suffering of the planet. The following story of Danny and Rita describes the true love of another son and his mother.

MOTHER AND CHILD

It was a snowy Christmas Eve when I got the first phone call from Rita. Her son Danny, who was suffering with AIDS, was in the midst of a pain crisis and she didn't know what to do. I made an emergency visit to their tiny home and found Danny in a fetal position on the corner of his bed, whimpering and moaning in severe pain. Rita, crippled with arthritis, was in a wheelchair in the living room, sobbing helplessly. Danny was 25 years old at the time, pale and thin, fragile and frightened. I encouraged him to take an extra dose of pain medication and sat with him until he was able to speak. He desperately needed to tell someone his story and became increasingly animated and impassioned as I listened.

He told me that his father had abandoned the family before Danny and his two younger brothers had even entered elementary school. Rita, with little education and no skills, had worked two jobs to support her sons. She had often gone without adequate sleep or food in her determination to provide for her children. Rita also looked after her sons' spiritual needs by taking them to church when she could and arranging for a neighbor to drive them when she was working. Danny remembered feeling loved and happy as a boy, though life was very hard for his family.

But everything changed when he became a teenager. At the age of fourteen Danny was sexually molested by the male neighbor who had been like a surrogate father to him. Ashamed and confused about his own sexuality, Danny couldn't tell his mother what had happened. He stopped going to church and began to experiment with drugs and alcohol to try to numb his guilt and shame.

Finally when he turned eighteen, Danny left home for a nearby city, cutting off all ties with his mother and brothers. He feared that Rita would be devastated if she knew the kinds of questions he was struggling with internally. He also did not want her to feel guilty for entrusting his care to the next-door neighbor for so many years. Danny chose to live all alone in the big city, supporting himself by becoming a male prostitute and continuing to use street drugs to keep himself from feeling his pain.

Several years later when he developed a cough and some lesions on his skin, Danny suspected that he had developed AIDS. He went to a clinic where a blood test confirmed the presence of the human immunodeficiency virus. Although he was offered free treatment for this condition, Danny left without seeing the doctor. He believed he was being punished for the lifestyle he was living and that he deserved to die from AIDS. Separated from his family and his soul, Danny was totally alone in this moment of crisis.

But a few weeks later, while walking down a busy city street, Danny ran into his cousin whom he had not seen since leaving home. This cousin revealed that Danny's younger brothers had both gone off on their own and his mother was now living alone. She had developed severe arthritis and had recently become confined to a wheelchair, but had no one to help care for her. Danny's heart broke open at the thought that his dear mother, who had given her life to raise him and his brothers, was now alone and suffering. Forgetting his own misery, he immediately packed up his few belongings and went home.

The reunion between Danny and his mother had taken place during the spring before I met them. Rita had been overjoyed to see her long lost son, an event she had prayed for since the day he left home. Danny said nothing to Rita about his own condition as he set about taking care of her, using the funds from a small savings account she had kept for him in case he ever returned. He filled her refrigerator with food and cleaned her house. He enlisted the help of some neighborhood boys to build a wheelchair ramp out the back door so she could get to and from her car in the driveway. He took her to a specialist to see if anything else could be done for her arthritis. For several weeks he showered Rita with the same kind of loving care that she had given to him throughout his childhood. He even drove her to church on Sundays, though he refused to attend himself. Rita had never been so happy.

In the early summer, while gazing out the front window, Rita mentioned to Danny how much she missed having a flower garden in the front yard. She had always enjoyed looking out and seeing the beautiful colors shimmering in the sunlight. Later that day Danny came home with trays and trays of summer flowers: pansies, marigolds, petunias and geraniums. He wheeled Rita outside where she could supervise while he planted them all. He even dug holes and handed her some of the plants to place in the soil so that she could feel the joy of gardening again. When the day was done, Danny had not only filled her little flowerbed with color but he had also lined the fence surrounding the entire yard with beautiful blossoms. Rita cried with joy and sat in front of the window staring at her flowers until she could no longer see them when darkness fell. She couldn't believe that her life was being so blessed.

But the intense work of the previous weeks began to take a toll on Danny's health. He developed fevers and had difficulty getting out of bed due to exhaustion. Finally he had to tell Rita his story, even though he was fearful of hurting her. Now it was Rita's turn, once again, to provide the loving tenderness her son needed. She expressed not one word of doubt or blame toward Danny and simply listened to him with love in her heart. Rita went with Danny to see an infectious disease specialist who diagnosed pneumonia and esophagitis and began treating him with appropriate medications. However, this same doctor had to deliver the bad news that Danny's AIDS had progressed too far to respond to treatment and he would not recover. Within a few more months Danny was admitted to our hospice for end-of-life care and this eventually led to my visit with him that Christmas Eve.

With some adjustments in his pain medication Danny became comfortable again and able to get out of bed for a few hours a day. Rita was constantly at his side, tending to him and showering him with her love. She prayed for Danny every day, in spite of the fact that he wanted nothing to do with God or church. Although it had worked well to that point for Danny to be home with his mother, our hospice staff had concerns that Rita, confined to her wheelchair, would not be able to care for him when he became totally bedridden. We held a meeting with the two of them to discuss options, such as placing Danny in a nursing home when that time arrived. Rita was adamant that she would not allow that to happen, so we left the subject alone, knowing that she would have to face it eventually.

However, the next time our nurse went to their home for a visit she found Rita standing up in the kitchen as she prepared soup for Danny's lunch. Much to the surprise of the nurse, Rita announced that she had been practicing walking ever since our meeting the week before. She had made up her mind to do anything it took to keep Danny at home with her, and so she had started by standing and taking a few steps in spite of the pain and weakness in her legs. Each day she walked a little farther and stood on her feet a little longer, until she was able to be out of her chair more hours a day than she was in it. She was determined, by the strength of her motherly love, to be Danny's caregiver in her home until he passed away.

And that is exactly what happened. As Danny grew weaker from his illness, Rita grew stronger, both physically and emotionally. When Danny became too frail to get out of bed she helped the home health aide bathe him and get him dressed every morning. She prepared special foods for him to eat, kept track of his medications, massaged his back and neck, and played his favorite music on the stereo. Each time our staff members visited the home they were amazed by the change in Rita. Driven by her intense love for her son, she continued to grow stronger and more active every week, in much the same way Danny had rebounded from his illness the previous spring to care for her. All the while Rita kept praying for Danny, although he refused to speak with her about God or the church.

Then early one Sunday morning Rita was awakened by a gentle tap on the shoulder. She was shocked to see Danny standing next to her bed, but he reassured her that for some reason he was feeling quite strong that day. He said only, "I want to go to church today." Rita asked no questions. She got dressed quickly after she helped Danny put on a shirt and some slacks. She wasn't sure he could really withstand an hour-long service, but she knew he was determined to do this and she would be there to support him, no matter what happened. Danny sat through the entire program. He was obviously in pain and very weak, but he seemed happy to be there. When it was over, they remained seated in the pew, waiting for the crowd to thin out before getting up to leave. At that moment, a young man came over to introduce himself to Rita and Danny. "I'm Josh," he said, "and I wonder if I might be of some assistance to you." Puzzled, the mother and son just stared at him, not sure what to say. Josh went on to explain that he had recently lost his partner to AIDS and had cared for him at home until his death. Josh recognized the lesions of Kaposi's sarcoma on Danny's skin and could tell from his thin and wasted body that Danny, like his partner, would soon die from AIDS. After Josh helped an exhausted Danny get out to the car, Rita invited him to visit them at home the next day, uncertain of the meaning of this encounter.

Ultimately, Josh became a close friend of both Rita and Danny, stopping by every day to offer help or run errands. He could easily lift Danny's emaciated body with his strong arms and would carry him from the bedroom to the living room whenever he needed a change of scenery. Josh told Rita and Danny that they were helping heal his grief by allowing him to be of service to them.

When I visited Danny for the last time, shortly before his death, Josh was there at his bedside, holding Rita's hand and providing strong and loving support to both Rita and Danny. When Rita and Josh left the room so I could listen to Danny's heart and lungs, Danny whispered to me, "Mom has a new son now." I searched his face, wondering if he felt jealous or threatened by this new relationship. But his eyes were shining as he spoke and his face was glowing with a beautiful soft light. "I don't have to worry about her anymore, do I?" "No, Danny. No, you don't have to worry about her." Sighing peacefully, Danny closed his eyes and drifted off to sleep.

Indeed, Josh did play the role of a surrogate son for Rita. He was there constantly through the final days of Danny's life and helped make the necessary funeral arrangements. The friendship between Rita and Josh continued on for several years as Josh frequently checked in to see if Rita needed anything. When love is great, such as the love between a mother and her son, it can overcome any obstacle. In fact, love can fill all the empty spaces, support the weakest limbs, inspire the hopeless soul; and, after breaking our hearts, love can finally help them heal again.

THE SEEDS OF LOVE

In the story of Rita and Danny we get a glimpse of true love in action: a love between a mother and son so intense that their hearts break open when they behold the suffering of the other. And, in return, each of them is healed by allowing the breaking that comes with love. We can interpret from the Bible that Jesus loved His own mother with that same intensity, permitting His heart to be broken, and that this is a model for each of us to learn how we are to love.

In his book *Grace and Grit*, Ken Wilber chronicles the death of his wife Treya from breast cancer. He describes her search for healing and her ultimate physical decline, throughout which she worked tirelessly on her own spiritual growth. Ken was Treya's caregiver during those years, broken open by his love for her and eventually achieving his own spiritual transcendence. While Treya was transformed by her struggle with illness and dying, Ken was transformed by being of service to her during her suffering. Ken writes of the breaking of the heart by love: "Real love hurts; real love makes you totally vulnerable and open; real love will take you far beyond yourself, and therefore, real love will devastate you."[10]

The lesson we are asked to learn from the dying is to Let Your Heart Be Broken, and the following are the seeds, the components, of love that we must grasp if we are to master this concept.

Relationships are Essential

In working with dying patients and their families, it quickly becomes clear that the relationships we form in life are the slate upon which we write the lessons of love. In order to explore the depths of love and truly become broken by love, we must share a mutual bond with some living thing, whether it is a person or even an animal. We must give ourselves totally to the other, risking our own safety and comfort, knowing all the while that we will be devastated some day in the future.

Of the dying patients who were part of our hospice, a few had no close family members or friends in their lives, and for them a pet often served as an object of deep love. In one instance a cherished cat was so closely attached to her owner that she laid next to him on his deathbed for two solid weeks, leaving only to eat small amounts of food or use the litter box. Another terminally ill patient owned a parakeet that perched on her shoulder for hours at a time during her final days, guarding the woman closely until she finally passed away.

But there were also those patients who had avoided all types of relationships and isolated themselves over time, and these individuals often suffered greatly from loneliness at the end of life. While they had spared themselves the broken-heartedness of love during this lifetime, they had also denied themselves the deep peace and comfort that comes after years of true love. Ultimately, many of those patients were eventually able to form bonds with hospice staff members or volunteers who came to care for them, finally having someone in their life who was willing to be of service to them. In this way, even those who had rejected love managed to experience a trace of it during their final hours.

An important fact is that each relationship offered to us during our lifetime has a purpose. Our connections with others serve as catalysts and supports for our spiritual growth. We must allow ourselves to become vulnerable within those relationships if we are to glean the "full harvest" they offer. Also, some of us may be seeking romance in our lives, hoping for a special partner who fulfills our dreams. But romance is not the same as true love and the loving relationships that end up transforming our lives may be very different than the love affairs of our imaginations. We must begin by genuinely loving those who are in our lives right now and focusing our energy there, rather than seeking a fantasy outside ourselves.

Connect Rather than Collect

During my years of hospice work I had the privilege of visiting patients in their own homes where I was able to observe their day-to-day life first-hand. I made calls to every imaginable type of dwelling, from a dingy studio apartment in the basement of a rundown building to an elegant Colonial house with a meticulously landscaped lawn. No matter the size or condition of the home, I found that the personality and values of the patient and family were reflected inside those walls by the possessions they cherished. Many patients had been collectors during their lives of all sorts of memorabilia, from silver teaspoons to porcelain dolls to antique cars, and on my visit to the home I was usually treated to a tour of the collection by a family member. I discovered, however, that the patients I had come to see had little interest in talking to me about their possessions. In fact, some of them dismissed my questions with a wave of the hand, stating, "I don't care about that anymore." Repeatedly I was reminded that at the end of life connections are more important than collections, as shown in the following story.

*   *   *

Ted was a former banker who was now in his 60s and dying from pancreatic cancer. When I first visited him in the enormous mansion where he lived, he showed me around and pointed out his many possessions, of which he had always been very proud. He talked at length about his expensive furniture, nice cars in the garage, his second home in the mountains, and the many achievements of his career. Clearly he had accomplished a lot in his lifetime and had reason to be pleased with himself, yet in that moment Ted exhibited an overwhelming sadness. He was beginning to struggle with the fact that his material wealth and success in life had always mattered more to him than anything else, including the people he had known. Now, none of his possessions could even begin to fill the emptiness he was feeling inside.

A few weeks later Ted was able to put this realization into words. Lying in a hospital bed, barely able to sip water, he held my hand tightly and said, "The only thing that matters is love. Who did I love? How much did I love them? How did I show that I loved them?" To his great remorse, he could only answer that he had loved no one. With urgency in his voice, Ted wanted me to understand what he was finally able to see. It was simply that love is what really matters. If you have love, you have everything; your life is complete. Ted told me on that day, from his new perspective, he would trade every accomplishment and every possession for just one more opportunity to give and receive love. His regret and sorrow were palpable, for this was a very painful lesson to learn.

Thankfully, however, Ted's final wish was fulfilled when his son, who had been estranged from him for many years, returned home just before his death. Ted was given one last chance to form an important connection and give away his love.

* * *

Ted's story clearly conveys the message that in the final analysis, the people we love are more important than the possessions we have amassed. However, in our society there is a common preoccupation with obtaining financial prosperity and acquiring more and more material belongings as a means of finding happiness. But the excessive pursuit of money and property in order to live a lifestyle just like Ted's can become a distraction from the path of spiritual growth. The painful emptiness we perceive internally is actually a call to develop as spiritual beings and learn to love. Too frequently we try to fill that gap with shallow and meaningless "things" and fail to find our way to genuine love.

While there is nothing wrong with setting a goal of wealth and prosperity, be careful to include the riches of genuine love in your plans for the future. Do not become so seduced by the lure of money and possessions that you neglect your opportunities to form deep connections with others in your daily life. In your last hours a fancy sports car will be no comfort when you long for a hand to hold or a shoulder to lean upon; your memories of business success will seem futile if you have no one to whisper "I love you" in your ear; and the size of your bank account will not soothe the ache of your suffering if you are all alone.

Love in the Small Things

Many times while working with hospice patients I witnessed the truth that the smallest act of loving-kindness can convey the greatest love. While some popular movies may portray enormous acts of courage as demonstrations of real love—walking across the frozen tundra of Siberia, navigating the Sahara desert, or rescuing a loved one from a sinking ship— the truth is that love is actually simple and is best conveyed through the insignificant moments of everyday life.

*　　*　　*

Sadie became our patient very late in the course of her battle with cancer. By the time we admitted her she already needed a hospital bed and was sleeping most of the day. Her husband Henry had taken a leave of absence from work in order to care for her full-time.

When I made my visit to their home, Sadie and Henry had only a few days left on this Earth together. Sadie's hospital bed had been placed in the living room, partly because it fit there better than any other room in the house and also because Henry wanted her to be in the center of activity where she could see and hear everything that was going on. I noticed immediately that Henry must have cleaned the house before my visit. Everything was neat and in its place, a condition that is often difficult to achieve when there is an ill person in the home. Henry provided me with the details of Sadie's illness and stories of her life, since she was unable to communicate with me herself. His great love for her shone through every word he spoke as he tenderly stroked her hair and hands during our conversation.

When I leaned over to listen to Sadie's heart, I was totally surprised to notice that she was wearing fresh lipstick and rouge! I looked up without saying anything and Henry explained, "Sadie has always been a beautiful woman and very careful with her appearance. I knew that she would never go to a doctor's appointment without wearing her makeup and I wanted her to feel comfortable while you were here, so I put it on for her." Tears stung my eyes and I was too moved to respond, when Henry added, "You know it's kinda hard to get lipstick on straight. I had to practice several times."

The depth of Henry's love for Sadie and his willingness to do anything for her spoke directly to my soul. I knew that I was in the presence of genuine, heart-breaking love and I stood in awe as Henry continued talking. He described something that had happened just the night before. He had been overcome with sadness at the thought of losing Sadie and had climbed onto the hospital bed next to her. Sobbing into the pillow, he cradled her body close to him for perhaps the last time. In the midst of his crying, he felt Sadie's hand touching him, patting his shoulder in a gesture of comfort, even though she was deep in a coma. Henry slept there the rest of the night in a tender embrace with his beloved Sadie, heartbroken and courageous in his practice of true love.

*   *   *

You see, true love is manifested in each and every moment by the little things we do, the attention we pay to the needs of the other, the openheartedness with which we give whatever is required in that single moment. True love can reveal itself through any action: stirring a pot of soup, folding a freshly laundered shirt, smiling at a stranger, picking up a piece of litter off the sidewalk. When we finally learn this lesson, we will understand how to infuse every moment of our lives with love.

Giving Before Receiving

True love manifests initially through the opening of our hearts and the act of giving to another person. When our initial action is to give away our love with genuine intention, then we are free to receive the natural flow of love in return. If we primarily seek to *be* loved or to *feel* loved, we have missed this opportunity to focus on what we can *give*. Love is an active verb, requiring us to put forth effort.

In the movie *Marvin's Room*, Diane Keaton portrays a woman named Bessie, who has spent all of her adult life caring for her bedridden father and elderly aunt. She has sacrificed her own goals and plans for her life in order to care for these two, and then she learns that she herself is dying of leukemia. When her estranged sister comes to visit, Bessie explains to her, "I've been so lucky to have Dad and Ruth. I've had such love in my life." Her sister replies, "They love you very much." "No," Bessie interjects. "I mean that I love them. I've been so lucky to have been able to love someone so much." We see once again that true love is found first by focusing on what can be given to others, risking the broken heart that follows when we lose the ones we have loved.

Once I observed an older male patient interacting with his daughter and granddaughter, who were his caregivers. Each time they tried to be of service to him, such as straightening his pillow or bringing him water, he shooed them away angrily. He told me, "I've always been independent and I don't like having people do things for me." I reminded him that he could give his family members a great gift by holding his desire for independence in check and allowing them to help him. I explained that caring for him as an act of love was part of their process of dealing with loss and grief. When he was finally able to understand that he had nothing left to give to them except his cooperation and gratitude for their service, he began to accept their loving gestures with thanks instead of anger, allowing true love to flow freely between them. When we utilize our energy to first give our love to others, we will certainly receive the return of that love in one form or another, even perhaps in surprising ways.

True Love Creates Miracles

Though the stories of breaking hearts and devastation make love sound formidable and undesirable, true love also has a delightful and whimsical aspect: the tendency for unexpected outcomes to occur when love is present. Whether you prefer to call them miracles or "extraordinary events," true love is a force that can generate powerful transformations. When love is the intentionality of a situation, a door opens to new possibilities. Synchronicities can flow and wonders can occur. Remember Rita leaving her wheelchair and walking again when Danny needed her care and Sadie who comforted Henry even though she was deep in a coma. The caveat is that miracles cannot be sought after as the goal of true love; they must be allowed to develop spontaneously. If we seek to attract a miracle to our lives, then our focus is on receiving rather than giving, and we have already seen that the giving of love must be the primary action. Even if we pray for a miracle to occur, such as the healing of an illness, the fact that all our energy is devoted to receiving the healing that is desired does not inspire the creativity of true love. To result in miracles, love must be given away first, without attachment or greed for what might be received in return, as illustrated by this next story.

*   *   *

I felt intimidated by Vernon from the moment I first met him. As a former Baptist minister he commanded great authority, in spite of being on oxygen and confined to his recliner in the family room. Vernon, though terminally ill, was passionate about his faith in God and did not hesitate to discuss theology, even upon the first visit of a stranger. When he was seventy years of age, still active in his church and preaching thundering sermons from his pulpit, Vernon had been diagnosed with lung cancer. He took a leave of absence from his ministerial duties to undergo extensive radiation therapy. He expected to bounce back quickly as he had done all of his life. But Vernon would never preach again. On the same day that he learned that the intense radiation therapy had completely rid his lungs of cancer he was also informed that the treatment had done irreparable damage to his heart muscle. In fact, most of his heart had been destroyed while the cancerous tissue in his lungs was being eliminated. This was the kind of "good news, bad news" irony that might have overwhelmed a lesser man. But Vernon, faith intact, understood that this was the path that had been put before him. He chose to follow with courage and dignity.

The damage to Vernon's heart had left him so weak that he could no longer walk to the bathroom without assistance. He ate his food very slowly because even chewing was tiring for him, and he slept a great deal during the day. Although he was no longer able to carry out his duties as a preacher, Vernon continued to read his Bible every day. He still loved to ponder theological issues and engage in discussions whenever he could gather the energy. He kept a spiral notebook on a table near his recliner and from time to time would jot down his thoughts or an idea, a practice he had always used when creating his sermons. The power of Vernon's faith was nearly palpable in his presence. When I spoke with him I found myself checking my words and thoughts for truthfulness and purity, just as if I were a schoolgirl in confirmation class.

But there was one thing that could rival Vernon's love of God. That was his devotion to his dear wife, Lydia. They had married in their early 20s, deeply in love and bonded so closely that it was as if they shared one heart. The love that united them had uplifted and supported Vernon over the years, giving him courage and inspiration for many of his powerful sermons. Vernon was now totally dependent on Lydia for his care and she worked tirelessly to make sure he stayed comfortable in his last days.

However, because of the severity of his heart disease, Vernon grew noticeably weaker every day. He soon was unable to walk at all and had to be lifted and transported in a wheelchair. Then he suffered a series of small strokes due to a lack of circulation to his brain. At that point he could no longer speak or communicate meaningfully with his family. Now unable to care for her husband by herself at home, Lydia faced the difficult task of admitting her dear Vernon to a nursing home. She cried for hours the day we brought him to the facility, her heart breaking at the thought that he would never return to their home again. Lydia spent most of her waking hours at Vernon's side, helping to feed and bathe him, devastated that she had not been able to care for him by herself. She brought his little table from home, along with his Bible, notebook, and pens. On his good days Vernon still managed to sit up and write in his precious notebook, though now his entries consisted of scribbles and chicken-scratches. When I visited him one day, he proudly showed me his notebook, turning to page after page of scribbles, where occasionally a decipherable letter or two would appear. I thought of the wonderful sermons Vernon must be composing in his mind, though he could never again share them with us.

A few days later, Vernon's condition declined further. He was now responding only briefly to those around him and sleeping nearly all the time. Lydia spent the day with him, but he did not awaken to greet her. When she grew weary that evening, she reluctantly said goodbye and kissed her dear husband on the cheek. But before she left the room she picked up his spiral notebook and turned to a new page, where she wrote "I love you, Vernon. Your Lydia." She placed the book gently on his chest, the pen still clipped to the page to hold it open.

Early the next morning Lydia received a call from Vernon's nurse. She had gone in to awaken him for his medication and found that he had died during the night. Lydia drove to the facility immediately, wanting to see her beloved partner and friend before the mortuary took his body away. Once there, she hugged and kissed him, straightening his blankets and squeezing his hands. Through her tears, she noticed his notebook sitting on the bedside table and picked it up to take home with her later. She gasped as she looked at the page where she had left her note the night before. There, underneath her writing, was line after line of Vernon's scribbles. This was followed by eight shaky, chicken-scratch letters, barely legible, but painstakingly copied from her note above: "I Love You." Vernon had indeed left his last message, as powerful as any sermon he had ever delivered.

*   *   *

Anything is possible when true love is present. We must allow our hearts to be broken in order to open the possibility for close relationships, small acts of great love, and everyday miracles to take place in our lives.

THE FRUITS OF LOVE

When you cultivate the act of sending true love out into the world, you will begin to receive the rewards of that practice, qualities that will enhance your life and help you on your journey out of suffering. Many of these qualities are contradictory to our instinctual human behavior and therefore take years and years of practice to develop. But they are the signposts of progress along the path of your spiritual growth and require your attention. As you toil in your spiritual garden here on Earth, love should be the fundamental focus of your energy and effort.

Vulnerability

Taking the risk to love another teaches you the art of vulnerability, opening yourself to the likelihood of being wounded. While your natural instinct is toward self-protection, love pushes you in the opposite direction toward more openness and greater risk. You become afraid to love when you have already been hurt by it, but love continues to call you forward, away from your defense mechanisms. When you are capable of being vulnerable you are also open to possibility. Miracles can occur, as in the stories of Danny and Rita, Henry and Sadie, and Vernon and Lydia. Rumi, a 13th century Sufi mystic and poet, wrote, "Your task is not to seek for love, but merely to seek and find all the barriers within yourself that you have built against it." You become vulnerable when you remove all your walls and obstacles, allowing you to grow and transform as you continue to learn how to love and be broken by love.

Authenticity

Once the barriers are taken down and you are able to become vulnerable, the next step in spiritual growth is to achieve authenticity, which is the quality of being fully trustworthy and real. However, authenticity is a difficult quality to find in our current society. The practice of marketing, which drives our economy and our culture to a large degree, is based on creating false impressions and shadowy half-truths, particularly fostering the notion that we are not complete unless we buy a certain product or service. We are bombarded on a daily basis with deceptive advertising and manipulative techniques through television and radio spots, billboards, direct mail promotions, Internet banners and pop-ups, and magazine and newspaper ads, to name a few. This practice of twisting the truth to promote a product or service is now so ubiquitous that it is accepted as a normal part of doing business in our society. But danger exists in the fact that because we are constantly inundated with lies, we are less able to recognize deception when it confronts us. In fact, we have the greatest difficulty seeing our own tendency to distort the truth within us.

However, true love can break open the shell of illusion and hypocrisy that surrounds us. True love is disarmingly real and authentic, as in Henry's simple act of applying Sadie's makeup or Vernon's careful copying of the words "I Love You." There is nothing artificial or fraudulent about true love, and when it is present it penetrates to the heart, stirring the recognition that this love is what really matters. True love demands honesty and will push you constantly in that direction, bringing up for your inspection all of the lies you tell to yourself and others. As a result, you will gradually grow in your own ability to be truthful and become better able to discern dishonesty when it is presented to you. Achieving authenticity requires dedication, for it is a quality that grows gradually over time, a product of much practicing of true love.

Selflessness

The quality of selflessness is also one that is difficult to find in our modern society. In fact, this nation is obsessed with the development of the self, as evidenced by the focus upon improving self-esteem, self-empowerment, individual rights, and self-motivation. The concept of selflessness may seem outdated and old-fashioned, but when you practice true love, you move naturally in the direction of placing your own individual needs below the needs of others. This is not to say that true love requires you to be downtrodden or abused, but rather that love elevates concern for others to a higher priority in your life. And as has been shown, when you do focus on giving love to others first, your own needs are met by the flow of love that returns to you.

As the practice of selflessness has disappeared from our American way of life, greed and narcissism have taken over. This has resulted in many of the ills with which we are now coping: the collapse of the stock market, hate crimes, increasing poverty, drug trafficking, gang violence, road rage and even such inconveniences as a lack of customer service throughout our society. Selflessness is a desperately needed quality in this world, but one that will require much cultivation before it can be harvested.

Compassion

When true love is practiced at the highest level, an awareness of and empathy for the suffering of others follows naturally. You develop the capacity to absorb the pain of your loved ones and exchange it for even more love, converting your own suffering in the process. In *Grace and Grit*, Ken Wilber describes this effect as it occurred during Treya's last months of life:

> "It was as if we were mutually generating in each other the enlightened compassion that we had both studied for so long. I felt like years, maybe lifetimes, of karma was being burned out of me in my continued response to her needs. And in her love and compassion for me, Treya also became completely full. There were no empty places in her soul, no corners left untouched by love, not a shadow in her heart."[11]

When true love leads to compassion practiced at this level, lives indeed transform and so might our society transform, as well. Love requires you to be of service to those who are suffering and you must count yourself fortunate whenever you are given this opportunity. There is no other way to develop compassion than to truly love those who are in your life right now, giving with authenticity, becoming vulnerable, and letting your heart be broken in the process.

THE VIEW FROM THE GARDEN

The love that you seek outside yourself is already part of you. Stop searching and begin giving love to everything around you: the tiny daisy struggling to grow through a crack in the sidewalk, the sparrow that lands on your windowsill, the homeless person on the street corner. Be courageous with your loving even though you fear being hurt. By giving away your love you open up space inside into which more love can flow in return. Be aware of the time and attention you devote to your possessions and reprioritize. Direct more energy to your relationships and less toward material goods. Cultivate compassion and selflessness toward others even if it causes you to be vulnerable. Remember that even the smallest acts can convey great love.

THE VIEW FROM THE GALAXY

When you take a look at love from the highest possible vantage point, an old Sunday school axiom becomes apparent: God is Love. This divinity is a light that permeates everything, everywhere—it is the creative energy that makes life possible. The true love that you practice in your life and give to others is a manifestation of the Divine in the world.

The breaking of your heart is necessary to allow the light of love to shine through more perfectly, illuminating the path that lies before you. When you can recognize this fact, then you cannot fail to participate in love, for you are made of love and breathe love in every moment. Only your hardheartedness prevents you from living love fully in your life. The light of love, radiating through your broken heart, enables you to see the Divine in others, to recognize their souls and connect with them in ways that can truly transform this world.

WHAT REALLY MATTERS ABOUT LOVE

Love illuminates the path that stretches before you.
Let your heart be broken to allow the light of love to
shine through.

LESSON 3

Forgiveness: HOLD NO RESENTMENTS

*"Father forgive them
for they know not what they are doing."*
-Luke 23:34

When we begin to experience true love for others in our lives, the next lesson we will be asked to learn is to "Hold No Resentments" by practicing Forgiveness, for love often requires forgiveness in order to be complete. This is another challenging lesson that many of us struggle to accomplish. But the act of forgiveness is so important that the entire life of Jesus was devoted to teaching it to us.

Jesus was born during a tribal era when vengeance and retribution were the dominant themes of behavior toward one's enemies, represented by "eye for eye, tooth for tooth." (Exodus 21:24) But Jesus came with an entirely different message: "Love your enemies," (Matthew 5:44); "Judge not, and you will not be judged; condemn not, and you will not be condemned; forgive, and you will be forgiven." (Luke 6:37) Jesus introduced the concept of a merciful God who offers forgiveness on a personal level to those who seek it, unlike the Old Testament belief in atonement that required a blood sacrifice. And Jesus also taught His followers to forgive one another, an idea that was totally revolutionary for the time.

But Jesus did not just teach others about forgiveness; He was called upon to practice it Himself, through His very human suffering. As He hung upon the cross, in the throes of agonizing death, He prayed for the forgiveness of His slayers. Jesus allowed them to end His life, fulfilling His destiny on earth, but held no resentments toward the men who carried out that course of action. This is the supreme act of forgiveness that we are asked to emulate in our own lives, no matter how difficult it seems or how far removed we are from accomplishing the task. Yet, as shown in the stories of the dying, at the hour of death (whether our own or that of a loved one) it is certain that we will be drawn and compelled to practice sweet, profound forgiveness. This is shown in the following story of Greg and his brothers.

BROTHERLY LOVE

Greg was the youngest of three sons in a hardworking family that ran an auto repair shop in a small town. His two older brothers were the favorites of their father and had always planned to take over the family business someday. Greg, whose birth was an "accident" that took place when his brothers were already in their early teens, was never close to them because of their age difference. Since he was more interested in music than cars, Greg bonded more closely with his mother Susan than with his father. However, when Greg was just eight years old Susan died tragically of malignant melanoma, leaving him feeling abandoned and bereft, with only his father and older brothers to raise him.

As might be expected, Greg had a difficult time getting his emotional needs met during those childhood years and his early life was filled with turmoil. He dropped out of school as an adolescent and began using drugs and stealing to support his habit. Eventually, he ran away from home and lived on the streets of a nearby city, in and out of jail, begging or stealing to buy drugs and food. Greg's brothers, David and Steve, were both married by that time, with their own children and living next door to one another in the small town where they had been raised. Both men were deeply religious and had no tolerance for Greg and his behavior. They cut off all contact with him and essentially disowned him for bringing shame to the family. When their father died a few years later, David and Steve did not even attempt to notify Greg, believing that he had broken the old man's heart. Both brothers expected that they would never see Greg again.

In fact, Greg disappeared from their lives for a number of years. However, one day when he was 28 years old, Greg showed up on David's doorstep out of the blue, saying simply, "I need help." Greg was dying of malignant melanoma, the very same type of cancer their mother had died from twenty years earlier. He was thin and bedraggled and was having difficulty breathing. The cancer had started with a lump under his right arm, exactly where his mother's cancer had started and had spread across his entire chest and into his right lung. Because he had no money or health insurance, and also because he was filled with self-hatred, Greg had not sought any medical care during his years away from home. Even when he recognized that he was seriously ill, he did not attempt to get treatment. By the time he arrived at David's house, his tumor was so widespread that nothing could be done to eradicate it.

David was so disgusted by the sight of his estranged brother standing on his porch that he started to shut the door in his face. But his wife Nancy welcomed Greg inside, stating, "We don't turn family away." Nancy transformed the guest bedroom into a sick-room for Greg and began caring for him, in spite of David's protests. She arranged for our hospice staff to help provide medical care for Greg and acquired a hospital bed and all the supplies she needed to dress his chest wound. David reluctantly agreed to allow Greg to stay in their home, but was filled with rage and resentment toward him, refusing to talk to Greg or be in the same room. And when Steve learned that his youngest brother was staying next door, he vowed never to visit, expressing his longstanding animosity, as well.

Greg was also intensely angry. He raged at God for the miserable life he had been given. He cursed his mother for leaving him and his father for not loving him enough. He made constant demands on Nancy, yelling if his food wasn't prepared properly, throwing things across the room, and waking her up repeatedly in the middle of the night to attend to his needs. While David threatened to throw Greg out of the house if his behavior persisted, Nancy quietly continued to care for him with loving-kindness. The cancer in his chest wall was growing rapidly, eroding through skin and subcutaneous tissue, creating purulent, foul-smelling drainage. Nancy had to change the dressing on his chest at least three times a day as the thick fluid rapidly saturated the gauze. Greg particularly hated these painful dressing changes and would shout and curse at Nancy every time she approached with fresh bandages. Yet she continued to give him impeccable care, seemingly tireless in her compassion and love for this irascible young patient.

For the first two weeks after Greg arrived there was so much anger and tension inside the house that Nancy would say she felt as if she were in the midst of a wildfire, surrounded by heat and destruction. Nevertheless, she maintained her soothing presence, blanketing the household with coolness and calm as she hoped the flames would extinguish themselves. Whenever hospice staff or volunteers arrived to help Nancy would pour out her sadness and pain, as she had no one else to give her support.

Then, a turning point occurred. Early one morning David found himself having difficulty sleeping, disturbed by an inexplicable restlessness. He lay awake next to Nancy, listening to her deep and sonorous breathing. She had collapsed into bed that night, exhausted from her care-giving duties. At some point David heard a noise in the hallway, followed by Greg calling out for help. He started to awaken his sleeping wife, but instead he allowed a trace of compassion to touch his heart and decided not to disturb her much needed rest. Reluctantly, David got out of bed and walked into the hallway outside his door. There he found Greg lying in a heap on the floor. He had tried to make it to the bathroom by himself, but was so weak he couldn't walk without support. David stood there for a moment, taking in the sight of his emaciated brother who was unable to move off the floor and was struggling to breathe. In that instant, David's heart broke open, freeing itself of the hardness and bitterness of the past years. David reached down and lifted Greg into his arms, shocked by the lightness of his body. He carried his little brother to the bathroom and then back to the hospital bed. With arms encircling one another at last, after so many years of pushing away, the two men were both deeply moved and filled with compassion and understanding toward each other. David sat by Greg's bedside the rest of the night. They talked softly, telling each other stories of the years they had been apart, each truly caring about the other for the first time in their lives.

But then, just as the sun was beginning to light the sky, there came a knock on David's front door. Their oldest brother, Steve, also unable to sleep that night in his home next door, had felt compelled to visit Greg one last time. Something intangible, beyond our knowing, had called those three brothers together that early summer morning. They spent the next few hours sharing stories and listening with open hearts. Eventually they cried together over their mother's death, healing three lifetimes of unresolved grief and pain.

When Nancy awoke that morning she could instantly feel that some-thing was different, that a great change had occurred within the home.

Throughout the following week David and Steve were frequently at Greg's bedside. The anger that had filled the household was mirac-ulously replaced with the warmth and glow of loving-kindness. When I visited the family at this point, Greg's gentleness and his brothers' concern touched me. Had Nancy not told me the story of what had occurred among them, I would never have suspected that these three brothers were once alienated from one another. When I asked Nancy what had happened to change the behaviors of the men, she replied simply, "They forgave one another."

Greg died at the end of that peaceful week, having experienced great relief from his pain and expressing no further anger or bitter-ness. He accepted his dying with grace and dignity, grateful to have known the love of his family if only for a few days at the end of his life. Nancy told me that David and Steve were transformed by the death of their little brother. They were grateful that Greg had come back into their lives and given them one last opportunity to heal the wounds that had separated them for so long, to let their hearts be broken open with love and finally, to forgive.

THE SEEDS OF FORGIVENESS

To understand the full extent of the lesson presented in the story of Greg and his brothers, and to appreciate the "seeds and fruits" of forgiveness, a clear definition of this process is necessary. Many times in my hospice work I met with patients who assured me that they had fully forgiven each wrongdoing that had been committed against them in their lives. And yet, these same patients could recite lists of people and events that had caused them harm while recalling every detail of the transgression. While they may have been living peacefully with those who had wounded them, they had not really accomplished forgiveness, but instead had offered only a truce or cease-fire. For these patients, flames of resentment and anger still burned internally and peace of mind and heart had never been attained.

Genuine forgiveness requires a shifting of one's energy away from hatred and blame toward healing and resolution. It is a concept that seems foreign to our rational minds. If someone wrongs us, we have an instinctual tendency to seek revenge, to ensure that punishment is carried out and that our idea of fairness is achieved. But the practice of forgiveness is motivated by love and the desire to make things whole, which is a difficult process that we must learn over the course of our lives.

Forgiveness is a Necessary Act of Love

When we truly love another person, we will inevitably arrive at a place where forgiveness is needed. For we are, at best, flawed human beings who make mistakes, act out our wounded anger, forget what really matters, behave badly, and ignore the needs of others. Relationships create a situation in which we must balance our own hopes and desires with those of another person and are therefore full of ups and downs, conflicts, and challenges. If we wish to maintain our relationships over time we will be forced to deal with imbalances and differences and will have many occasions in which to practice forgiveness. Ideally, our capacities for true love and profound forgiveness blossom simultaneously, side-by-side; then we will have an opportunity to experience the highest possible form of spiritual love.

In the last chapter we learned that love must be allowed to break us in order for us to fully manifest our divine potential. This current lesson will teach us that what has been torn apart by love can be bound together again by forgiveness. Forgiveness is a practice we should desire to cultivate in our lives, for ultimately it benefits the giver as much as the recipient. The Buddha taught that "Holding on to anger is like grasping a hot coal with the intent of throwing it at someone else; you are the one who gets burned." There is nothing gained from harboring ill will toward another and everything to gain from letting it go.

Forgiveness of Self

Forgiveness is an action that is generated internally and works to straighten out the tangles of resentment that have been carried over from the past. Eventually for each person forgiveness must be directed toward the self in order to move toward spiritual growth. The dying must confront head-on the frailty of their human bodies, the weaknesses of their character, and the disappointing failures of their life experience. Many of these patients, such as Greg in our story, rage in anger over the loss of physical health, disillusioned that life has followed such a seemingly negative course. But it is crucial that these patients, and all of us, manage to forgive the deterioration of the human body, for it was always meant to be this way from the moment of birth. Our bodies, and therefore our lives, carry within them the seeds of our mortality. If we cannot accept this and forgive ourselves we will not be able to move forward and forgive others.

In addition, over the course of a lifetime each of us accumulates our share of regrettable decisions and actions that require our own forgiveness. If we are able to look within ourselves with honesty we are likely to find a twisted mass of guilt and remorse hidden away in the depths. If we do not address this inner shadow, it will sabotage our efforts to transform ourselves by generating self-doubt, fear, and low self-esteem. We must clear away the blame we have harbored toward ourselves, untying those knots and straightening the threads. Many times the anger and wrath we direct toward others is really our own self-recrimination projected outward. We must first heal this self-hatred before we can accurately assess the actions of those around us. When we bring those shadowy parts of ourselves into the light of love we will be able to see more clearly, experience compassion, and soothe our self-inflicted wounds.

Forgiveness of Others

Next, we must direct the power of forgiveness outward toward those who have wronged us in our lifetime. We have to make a conscious decision to let go of resentment and create internal peace. To accomplish this we will wrestle with the rational mind, which cannot perceive a benefit in forgiving another. However, over time our ability to forgive will evolve and grow as we develop spiritually.

One couple I worked with through hospice had lost a child many years in the past in an automobile accident caused by a drunk driver. They described the accident to me with much sadness, but I could detect no anger or hatred in them. Though they grieved the loss of their son deeply, they had chosen to forgive the man who was responsible for his death. They told me it had taken them many years to reach this point of inner peace, but that remaining angry would have been destructive to them. Forgiveness was part of their commitment to continue living even without the son they cherished. Their sorrow was sweet and poignant because it was not distorted with resentment. And by practicing forgiveness they released themselves from the toxic effects of harboring ill will toward another person.

While forgiving someone for the loss of a child is one of the most challenging tasks imaginable, each of us will be asked in a manner unique to our own lives to experience loss and offer forgiveness. It is up to us to discover our own process of forgiving from the heart, starting wherever we find ourselves in life. Sometimes forgiveness requires a physical demonstration of love and compassion to serve as a catalyst for reconciliation. The following story is an example of a loving deed that opened hearts to forgiveness.

*   *   *

Emma was in her late 80s and dying from the complications of diabetes. She had moved in with one of her daughters when she became too ill to care for herself, sleeping in a little guest room in the back of the house. A second daughter lived nearby and helped share in her care.

Emma was bedridden due to damage to the nerves and blood vessels in her legs caused by her longstanding diabetes. She was declining rapidly from this disease that had also damaged her kidneys and heart. She tried to prepare herself for death by saying goodbye to all her loved ones, especially to her daughters and grandchildren who were frequently at her bedside. But she also had a son, Bill, who had become estranged from the rest of the family. Many years in the past a disagreement between Bill and his sisters had resulted in his withdrawal from the entire family; he rarely saw Emma and never spoke to his sisters. When Bill learned of his mother's condition he began to stop by for occasional visits with her, but his sisters refused to acknowledge him, leaving the house as soon as he arrived. Emma agonized over this separation between her children and wondered how to heal their anger, but none of them would discuss the situation with her. However, as often occurs when a need arises, life itself provided a solution.

Emma had always been talented at handicrafts and needlework and frequently made gifts for her family and friends. She had started a tradition of creating a hooked rug for each of her grandchildren and great-grandchildren after they were born, each bearing the child's name and birth-date in bright colors and designs. Her most recent great-grandchild had been born just before she moved into her daughter's home and Emma had started making a rug for the baby right away. She had worked on it a little every day even though she was very tired much of the time. However, when the project was only half completed, Emma had to abandon it altogether. Her hands had become too weak and her eyes too dim to manipulate the latch hook and small pieces of yarn.

Emma entered into a state of depression, feeling hopeless because she was unable to accomplish the tasks she needed to complete before dying. She had wanted to finish making the rug, but, more importantly, she had hoped for reconciliation between her children. In despair, Emma withdrew from her family for several days and spent most of her time sleeping. Her daughters believed that this retreat into seclusion was just a normal stage of the dying process, but Bill decided to ask Emma what she was feeling. She described for him her disappointment over the rug and her children's estrangement as Bill listened in silence. After hearing everything Emma had to say, Bill left the house and disappeared for a few days. This confused Emma and caused her to become even more despondent. Her daughters, still angry with Bill, viewed his behavior as typically irresponsible and uncaring, and they were even more determined never to forgive him.

However, after three days Bill did return, and in an instant, everything changed. He was carrying with him a shopping bag and seemed quite excited about whatever he was hiding inside. This time his curious sisters decided to stay in the house during his visit to find out what was going on. As he sat on the bed next to Emma, Bill pulled from the bag the hooked rug Emma had been making for her great-grandchild. But rather than the half-finished project Emma had put away a few weeks earlier, he held up for her a fully completed rug with every piece of yarn perfectly in place. Bill had somehow finished it for his mother himself, struggling to coordinate the small bits of colored yarn and delicate latchet hook with his large hands that were stiff and gnarled from years of manual labor. Emma cried with gratitude at such an act of love from her son. Her daughters looked on with amazement, overwhelmed by this showing of tenderness and compassion from their hard-hearted brother. This moment was the beginning of the reconciliation for which Emma had prayed. Starting then, her three children managed to forgive one another and be together at her bedside when she died, just as she had hoped.

*   *   *

This story is a beautiful illustration that forgiveness is sometimes precipitated by an act that demonstrates great love and courage. Bill completed the rug, something he had never done before, out of pure love for his mother and a desire to ease her pain. Witnessing this demonstration of love, his sisters' hearts were opened and they were finally able to do the work of forgiveness. In a similar way in Greg's story at the beginning of this chapter, David's reaching down to lift Greg off the floor and carry him in his arms was the physical demonstration of love that opened all their hearts and made forgiveness possible. As another act of love, Nancy had devoted many selfless hours to caring for Greg's needs, absorbing all the rage and resentment that had built up around him and setting the stage for transformation to occur. Whether inspired by a change in attitude or an act of love, forgiveness of others is a crucial step that allows us to proceed on our journey toward spiritual growth.

Forgiveness of God

While the traditional religious view of forgiveness is that it is a merciful gift bestowed upon mankind by God, many of the dying patients I have cared for have struggled with a need to offer their own forgiveness to God whom they blamed for their pain. Encountering serious illness at a young age, enduring prolonged or severe suffering, or experiencing multiple losses, are all factors that can lead to anger and resentment toward God. Forgiving God may be the most difficult task of all for some, because God is not visible and tangible to them. But hatred of God is poison to the soul and must be resolved, no matter how long it takes.

*   *   *

John, who was just 30 years old, was dying of esophageal cancer after a two-year battle. He had two small children and was devastated at the thought of leaving them. He spent many hours in discussions with his wife and various counselors from his church trying to make peace with his death. His family told me that he had been able to prepare himself well and say goodbye to everyone significant in his life.

He had even called a former friend with whom he had quarreled in the past and reconciled their differences. At that point, John announced that he was ready to die. He soon lapsed into a coma and began the process we refer to as "active dying." Usually this stage lasts only a few days to a week, depending on several factors. But John had been lingering in this state for over two weeks, defying medical logic. Something seemed to be keeping him here; something was unfinished in his life.

When I went to visit John he was in the semi-comatose state that precedes death. He was not responsive most of the time, but could hear our voices and could choose to react when the need arose. In this state it was as if his spirit was engaged in a faraway place, but could still return to us when necessary. He seemed agitated at times, unable to rest deeply, with tension evident on his face.

John's wife and I talked at length about any possible issues that could be unfinished for him and keeping him here. He had written letters to his two children that were to be opened by them when they were old enough to understand. He had said goodbye to everyone important in his life. His wife could think of no other issues that might need resolution before John could die peacefully.

Finally I spoke to John. Holding his hand, I told him I wondered if there was something he needed to do or know before he could die. I began to ask specific questions to see if any would draw a response from him. I could detect no reaction at all until I asked, "John, have you forgiven God?" This was a question I knew to ask because of my experiences with other patients. Suddenly he squeezed my hand tightly and opened his eyes, which flashed with rage. He continued to stare at me intently while I talked about his need to let go of anger at God. I told him it wasn't fair at all that he was dying at such a young age, but that there is wisdom in this world and in our lives that far surpasses our understanding. He continued to squeeze my hand and stare at me while I spoke. Then, tears began to pour down his cheeks as he finally relaxed his grip, rested his head on the pillow and closed his eyes. He remained deep in a coma through the night and died peacefully the next morning.

*   *   *

Coming to terms with our own concept of God is necessary for each of us in order to achieve a peaceful end of life. Even those who have no particular belief system or faith need to encounter Fate or Luck or Chance, or whatever they perceive to be the dominant force in the Universe, and resolve the disappointment and anger they feel. This is a fundamental task of our human existence that, if accomplished earlier in life, can benefit us greatly. Once when I presented this information to a group at a local Senior Center an elderly woman raised her hand and asked, "How do you forgive God when he takes innocent people away? My husband begged God every night to let him live longer and God didn't answer his prayer. Now how am I supposed to forgive a God like that?" Her anger was visible and her suffering was great. In her view her husband's death appeared totally unfair and God seemed to deserve the blame. Her own life was now ravaged with bitterness because of a lack of acceptance of and appreciation for our human mortality. As is true for all of us, this woman needed to let go of her rage and allow herself to see from a new perspective before she could begin to heal.

At times our resentment and anger toward others, including God, may be buried deep inside, hidden underneath layers of grief and shame. In order to achieve true forgiveness we must unearth our suffering, face it with courage and honesty, and gradually open our hearts to release resentment. This is indeed a process that can require a lifetime to accomplish. For many of us the urgency of dying is the only impetus strong enough to push us to heal these wounds, but it is time to begin this work now in order to move forward toward the consciousness that may change the world.

Forgiveness Heals

"Forgiveness is the means for taking what is broken and making it whole."

-Robin Casarjian

This message cannot be overemphasized: the act of forgiveness has a profound effect on physical, mental, emotional, and spiritual health. Releasing long-held resentments frees up energy that has been stored in the wound and provides opportunities for healing and growth. Most frequently I have witnessed the healing of relationships through the act of forgiveness, as in the story of Greg and his brothers and that of Emma's children. But occasionally forgiveness leads to a miracle of physical healing as well, as shown by the following story.

*   *   *

Glenda was nearly 50 years old when she was diagnosed with ovarian cancer. Never having been married, she lived alone in a simple house, relying on her many friends for social and emotional support. She underwent diagnostic testing to determine the stage of her cancer, but decided, in the end, to refuse all treatment. At that point she was admitted to our hospice with a prognosis from her oncologist of less than six months to live. Our staff found Glenda to be a beautiful, gracious woman, who expressed a peaceful willingness to accept her own death if it was truly the right time for her to die. She was quiet and pleasant, always grateful for the visits and care that were offered to her. As the months passed, however, Glenda's physical condition never seemed to deteriorate. She required no pain medications and all her organ systems seemed to be functioning normally.

After a full year had passed her insurance company stopped paying for hospice services because her health was showing no decline. She revisited her oncologist who was shocked to see her looking so well. Diagnostic tests were repeated and indicated no evidence of the cancer that had been raging in her body the previous year. When I visited Glenda one last time in order to close our files and discharge her from our care, I asked her how this miracle had occurred, wanting to learn from her experience. She said simply, "I forgave everyone." She went on to tell me that she spent each day focusing on forgiving every person who had ever harmed her. When she had completed that task she continued to extend forgiveness to anyone toward whom she held even slight negativity, including people she did not know personally, such as political figures and criminals she had read about in the news. Glenda's ritual of forgiveness was so powerful that her body had been healed by the practice, though she had never asked for blessings for herself or focused attention on her own needs. Glenda exuded peace and serenity that day as we spoke and I could feel the strength of her compassion. She had achieved a calmness of spirit that had healed her body and could potentially heal the planet, as well.

*   *   *

In Glenda's story we see that forgiveness, just like love, is most powerful when the focus is on giving rather than receiving. Glenda wasn't seeking to heal her cancer by practicing forgiveness; she was forgiving others because it felt to her like the right thing to do. She was called to this act by her knowledge that her life was coming to an end and by her desire to create peace before she left this world. The fact that her body was healed was an amazing gift to her, particularly because she wasn't expecting it to happen. When such forgiveness is offered up freely in the world, miracles can occur and shifts in energy can be inspired. Each of us is called by our knowledge that life is fleeting, to become creators of change, practicing forgiveness to heal our world.

Forgiveness Transforms

The power of forgiveness to bring about change was demonstrated in the story of Greg's family as we saw how the stored anger and grief of three brothers was transformed in a single morning. Not only was each of these brothers changed by the experience of forgiveness, but their memories of the past were altered as well. David and Steve no longer saw Greg as the shameful "black sheep" of the family because their view of him had expanded to reveal a grief-stricken, lonely little boy whose agony turned into rage and destructive behavior when he grew up. Greg could see the pain and helplessness of his brothers and could no longer blame them for his own torment. In the moment that their hearts broke open to one another the resentment and bitterness melted away, leaving pure compassion in its wake. From this perspective, it was no coincidence that Greg's cancer was the same type and had occurred in the same location as the cancer that took their mother's life. Unhealed grief over the traumatic loss of their mother had been the major cause of anger and resentment for each of the brothers. Perhaps the opportunity to relive her death through Greg's illness was the impetus required for the three brothers to finally heal. In this way, Greg had been able to see meaning in his own life and death, knowing that his presence on this earth had been a profound blessing to his older bothers. This knowledge brought a peaceful end to his ravaged life.

There are other powerful examples of transformative forgiveness that have occurred in our recent past. In October of 1998 a tragic murder took place near Laramie, Wyoming. Matthew Shephard, a 21-year-old young man who was openly gay, was brutally attacked and beaten by two other men. He was then tied to a fence, arms outstretched, and left to die. Following news of his horrific death our nation and much of the world were stunned by this display of man's capacity for cruelty and hatred. But Matthew's parents, though devastated by their own grief, advocated against the death penalty for one of the murderers, offering him a chance for life that had been denied to their son. They went on to form a foundation in Matthew's name and worked to end hate crimes and spread forgiveness throughout society.[12] The world cannot help but be transformed by such an act of forgiveness offered freely by parents who were surely broken-hearted.

In October of 2006, just eight years after Matthew Shephard's death, a gunman entered a one-room Amish schoolhouse in Nickel Mines, Pennsylvania to take ten young schoolgirls, ages 6 through13, as hostages. He eventually shot all ten of the girls, killing five of them before taking his own life. The reaction of the Amish community, while overwhelmed with their own loss, was to reach out to the family of the shooter within hours after the tragedy to offer them messages of forgiveness and support. They also set up a charitable fund for that family, attended his funeral, and invited his widow to attend the private funeral services for their perished daughters. This astonishing act of total forgiveness helped heal their own grief and allowed the family of the shooter to heal as well, demonstrating to the world the miraculous power of refusing to hold resentments toward another, a value rooted deeply in Amish culture. A short time later the ill-fated schoolhouse was demolished. A new classroom was erected nearby and renamed The New Hope School, completing on a physical level the transformative act of forgiveness.[13] Thus tragedy, when embraced and forgiven with a heart broken open, can offer up New Hope, indeed.

When we follow the path of forgiveness we will be led to deeper and more painful challenges. If we choose to live a life that focuses always on forgiveness, then we must commit to viewing every situation with an open heart. When a bomb destroys a building and hundreds of lives are taken, we must be prepared to forgive the person who made and planted the deadly bomb. When a young child is kidnapped and murdered, we must be able to forgive the murderer, to forgive the parents who could not protect the child, and to forgive the God who allowed such a tragedy to occur. When a doctor is shot and killed after performing an abortion, we are called to forgive the shooter for his act, to forgive the doctor for performing the abortion, and to forgive the woman who sought the abortion. When our life force begins to slip away and our body becomes frail and aching and useless, we must be ready to forgive our Creator for our mortality. The task of forgiveness can be as big as the entire Universe, requiring a lifetime to accomplish, but bringing blessings and treasures to us along the way.

THE FRUITS OF FORGIVENESS

The choice to live a life guided by forgiveness, while difficult to follow, can lead you to harvest many other benefits. By learning and practicing this lesson now rather than waiting until the end of life you can advance your growth as a spiritual being, awakening further into consciousness and discovering the true secrets of the life you were meant to live.

Responsibility

When you truly practice forgiveness toward yourself and others your ability to take responsibility for your own actions will be tremendously enhanced. Once you look within your own Shadow and clear away the knots and tangles of past misdeeds you will clear a space for the light of love, enabling you to evaluate your current behavior more accurately. Taking responsibility for your conduct will require you to settle your wrongdoings toward others more quickly and will result in more thoughtful choices in the future. From a position of responsibility you will be able to navigate your life toward a higher path rather than wallowing in the mud of victimization. Practicing forgiveness removes some of the major obstacles to your spiritual growth, allowing you to proceed toward greater awareness.

Tolerance

In the stories of the dying presented in this chapter, each of the people who found their way to forgiveness also discovered an increased capacity for tolerance toward others. This ability to empathize with those whose beliefs and practices differ from your own becomes extremely valuable to you as you work your way through all the challenges of life. When you become more spiritually conscious in the world you will also become more aware of the suffering of others, the injustice and wrongdoing that exists around you, and the diversity of people and perspectives on this planet. In order to promote peace and accord in this world you must be tolerant of others, patient with their shortcomings, and able to see beyond their limitations. An open heart that readily embraces forgiveness finds a direct route to tolerance for all others.

Reconciliation

Reconciliation, the act of resolving conflict with others, also follows naturally from the practice of forgiveness. Restoring relationships that had previously been damaged is immensely liberating to the soul, rec-reating connections with people of importance in your life. Just as the three brothers of the first story of this lesson, David, Steve, and Greg, basked in the calm and peaceful atmosphere that surrounded them after their moment of forgiveness, everyone can benefit from the joy of rec-onciliation that lifts away the burden of old anger and resentment. Even those who are outside the circle of reconciliation can sense and enjoy the serenity that follows from such an act, just as Nancy and our hospice staff instantly felt the change that took place in that household once the three brothers had forgiven one another. In addition, transforming painful, problematic relationships into supportive, loving connections is extremely beneficial to you as you navigate the difficulties of life. You thrive when surrounded by networks of positive bonds with others, uplifted and nurtured by those who share your life-space rather than burdened and exhausted by negative alliances.

Redemption

The next benefit that follows directly from forgiveness—and the reconciliation it creates—is the act of redemption. By creating some-thing beautiful from the ashes of a devastated life, redemption allows you to gain back what might have been lost before, such as family, connectedness, love, honor, and peace. Carrying grudges and bitterness toward others costs you energy as you keep those negative memories and emotions burning forever inside you. Once you are able to let go of those poisonous feelings trapped within, you experience a release of this energy and renewed inspiration for growth and learning. When you reclaim the damaged pieces of yourself that have been suspended in the past by keeping alive painful memories, you can move forward in the world as a whole being, fully functional, ready to transform and create new hope all around you, ready to heal this planet.

THE VIEW FROM THE GARDEN

The work of forgiveness requires constant awareness of your own interior world, including your reactions to things that happen to you, your self-beliefs, and your judgments of others. You must focus effort every day on being responsible for your own thoughts and actions and making amends for your behavior that falls short. Moreover, you must free others from the snares of your blame and resentment to heal your relationships and to allow transformation to occur. Extend your forgiveness toward your own physical existence and toward the Creator, whatever you perceive that force to be, in order to complete this task. Recognize that the practice of true love requires you to master forgiveness as well.

THE VIEW FROM THE GALAXY

"Forgiveness is the fragrance the violet sheds
on the heel that has crushed it."

-Attributed to Mark Twain

For a final look at forgiveness your must ascend to the highest point imaginable and take this lofty perspective: the ultimate goal of your spiritual existence is to Hold No Resentments, whatsoever, toward others. This means to offer immediate forgiveness to those who harm you as Christ forgave His slayers, as the Amish community reached out with compassion to the family of a murderer, and as the crushed violet blesses the one that tramples it with beautiful, fragrant forgiveness. Allow no thoughts of hatred or bitterness to remain within you, Release them in each and every moment as they arise to afford resentment no safe harbor in your heart or soul.

To achieve this highest possible manifestation of forgiveness you must begin seeing the world through "new eyes," recognizing that every event of your life has been perfect for you, exactly what has been required for your growth. This lofty spiritual perspective requires an understanding that nothing in your life is a mistake and no event a tragedy that should not have happened. To hold no resentments means seeing the promise and potential for growth in everything. And when the events of life are beyond your understanding and you cannot see the purpose or meaning in tragedy, you must simply hold on and trust that even in doubt there is perfection.

For it is the great irony of life that every tragedy contains the seeds of transformation that will bring healing. Christ's crucifixion redeems the lives of those who put him to death, Matthew Shephard's murder raises awareness that hatred must be transcended and transformed with love, an Amish community creates new hope through their simple act of profound forgiveness, and the violet leaves its fragrance upon the heel that has crushed it.

To share in this healing process, begin now to unravel the tangled threads of anger and loosen the knots of hatred residing within you. Reclaim your creative energy from the past and feel the burden lift from your heart as you open your eyes in this present moment. Resolve from this time forward to hold no resentments, no matter what is lost or what fate befalls you.

WHAT REALLY MATTERS ABOUT FORGIVENESS

Forgiveness removes the obstacles on the path of
spiritual growth.
Hold no resentments as you let go of the past and reclaim
your energy.

LESSON 4

Paradise: DWELL IN THE PRESENT MOMENT

*"Truly I say to you today,
you will be with me in Paradise."*

-Luke 23:43

When we begin to master the art of forgiveness we untie the knots of resentment and bitterness that have been keeping us attached to the past, allowing the release of life-giving energy. As we progress further on this path of spiritual growth that has been laid for us by the dying, we are asked to harness that life force and "Dwell in the Present Moment," finding our place in Paradise on Earth. One of the keys to understanding this lesson is found in the dual meaning of the word "dwell," which means to live or exist in a place and also to keep the attention focused upon something. To discover paradise we must live in the present by bringing our attention and energy to each moment.

Jesus spoke these words on the cross after He was asked by one of the thieves being crucified next to Him to "Remember me, my Lord, when you come in your Kingdom." The reply of Jesus contains not only a blessing of forgiveness for the man, but also a guarantee that the thief will be, today, in the present moment, in paradise along with Jesus. It is important to note that Jesus used the word "Paradise" and not "Heaven." The Aramaic interpretation of paradise is a beautiful garden, a place of harmony and tranquility and also a place where all of one's needs are met.[14] Paradise is then an earthly manifestation of Heaven, something available here and now, not far away in the sky and the future.

This promise of Jesus implies that paradise already exists, infusing us with abundance, even though we do not recognize it and must be reminded of it repeatedly. But paradise can only be experienced today, in this present moment, for it does not inhabit the past or the future. Our challenge is to dwell in and upon the present, bringing forward all our energy away from the knots of the past. Ironically, seeking outside ourselves for a Utopia, the form of paradise conjured up by our imaginations, only serves to blind us to the true paradise that lies within us. We must be patient and content in this very moment in order to awaken in Paradise. Consider the following story of Ralph, a simple man who found his own unique Paradise.

THE STUDENT DESK

The first time I visited Ralph I spent a few extra minutes sitting in the car in front of his apartment building, steeling my nerves and summoning the courage to walk inside. He lived in one of the worst parts of town in a tumbledown, three-story apartment complex whose address was frequently mentioned on police scanners as the location of a drug bust, robbery, or gang-related shooting. It was not really considered a safe place to visit, but it was my job to call on Ralph and assess his medical needs, and I was determined to carry it out. Besides, I had grown up in the poor section of my hometown, and the specter of poverty was not new to me. I believed I could handle whatever I found inside, so I bravely stepped from my car and into the doorway of the dilapidated structure.

There was only a small window in the front door of the building and the hallway was dimly lit. Before my eyes could adjust to the darkness my nose was assaulted with the smell of urine and stale cigarette smoke. Then I began to take in the visual details of this forbidding place. The dingy carpet had been worn through to the floorboards in some areas and was so filthy I could not identify its original color. Stained wallpaper peeling from the walls formed a broken arch over my head, its faded floral print suggesting that this place had held a more dignified existence at some time in the past. Constructed for greater purposes than were now apparent, the building, perhaps like the people who inhabited it, had been diminished to this state of ruin through years of hard use and neglect.

Squinting at the mailboxes on the wall, I read that Ralph lived in Apartment C. I made my way down the hallway, peering at each door, some without markings at all, some leaking the sounds of human voices, or the vibrations of rock music, or trails of cigarette smoke. At the end of the corridor I descended a narrow stairway to an even darker passage in the basement. At last, there was the "C" I had been searching for on a door left slightly ajar. I rapped lightly with my knuckle, but Ralph had already heard my footsteps and was calling me in, even as I knocked. The sight of his apartment, by that time, was no more shocking than the rest of the building had been. A single window facing out at ground level provided a dim light to the room. A small table beneath the windowsill was piled high with magazines, papers, medicine bottles, dishes, cigarette cartons, and other assorted items. In the corner of the main room a mattress covered with filthy, tangled sheets rested on the floor. The kitchen counter and sink were so filled with food-encrusted dishes that not even one more dirty glass could be placed there. Ralph was reclining in the apartment's only chair, an old upholstered rocker with foam stuffing bulging up here and there through its many rips and tears. He greeted me with genuine friendliness and urged me to "Sit down for a minute." I hesitated momentarily, scanning the room in hopes of finding another seating option, then gave in and plopped myself down on the edge of the mattress.

Ralph was a 60 year-old man who had been referred to hospice because he was dying of kidney failure caused by renal cancer and was not a candidate for dialysis. His physician speculated that he might live for two to three weeks and had asked us to make sure Ralph was comfortable at home since hospitalization would be expensive and he lacked health insurance. Fortunately, our hospice had a charitable fund for patients just like Ralph, so we were able to give him the care he needed free of charge.

It turned out that Ralph had led a pretty rough life. He had spent a little time in jail, though he did not elaborate on the crimes that had landed him there. He did admit to being homeless most of his life, living by the railroad tracks and scrounging through trash cans for food. I gathered that alcohol and drug abuse had also played a role in his history even though he didn't want to talk about that part of his life. His current living conditions were quite lavish in his eyes, with a roof over his head, a bed and a working refrigerator. All this was made possible by a very small pension he received because he had once worked for the railroad when he was younger.

A social worker in his oncologist's office had helped him qualify for this stipend that now covered his rent and paid for a small amount of food each month. Ralph's eyes danced as he described this good fortune, grateful for everything he had been given in these last days of his life. As I settled in and listened to his lively stories, I began to get a picture of a vagabond who had always lived unencumbered and with no attachments until disease had crept up on him to steal his carefree way of life.

Ralph talked easily and openly for quite some time about his past, his illness, and his experiences with doctors. He even seemed comfortable discussing his approaching death, showing no fear or regret. But when I asked him about his family he grew silent. He responded simply, "I have children, but we haven't seen each other for many years ... and that's for the best," smiling to indicate to me that he was at peace with that part of his past. Then, I gently asked Ralph if there was anyone around to help with his needs when he became too ill to care for himself. He answered that he had a friend, Ben, who lived upstairs in the apartment building and looked in on him every day. "I'll be OK," Ralph reassured me. He talked about his waning strength, how he could no longer take the long walks he used to enjoy or go fishing in the nearby river, and he admitted to being in a little pain, but he did not complain. In fact, he seemed to feel that he was a very fortunate man, living in what he could only describe as Paradise compared to the experiences of the rest of his life.

During the length of this visit I took the opportunity to look around Ralph's apartment a little more carefully. I noticed that there were pieces of notebook paper taped on each of the walls in various places. Since there was nothing else that could even be construed as decorative in the entire apartment, I wondered about these papers that Ralph had so carefully attached to his walls. Finally overcome by my curiosity, I rose to take a closer look and found that each piece of paper bore a pencil drawing of some outdoor scene. One was a mountain vista with cactus in the foreground; another was a train, winding its way along some lonesome tracks in the middle of a desolate prairie. Before I could look at Ralph to ask for an explanation, he gave me the answer, "I've decided to take up drawing. Since I can't do much now, I just started drawing pictures of some of the things I've seen in my life." My mouth dropped open as I studied these works of art painstakingly crafted with a number 2-pencil on sheets of ruled paper torn from a spiral notebook. Given the materials he had to work with the fine details of each drawing were amazing, with shading and contrast to highlight depth and perspective. Ralph was pleased with his work, but as with everything else he was quite humble and matter-of-fact about it. "Gives me something to do with my time." Indeed, he had been working on a sketch just before I arrived, and I could now see the work-in-progress on top of a large catalog he held in his lap as a drawing surface.

I was astounded and deeply touched. Here in this desolate, decrepit building in a room brimming with trash and filth and disarray, here in the dying of a man viewed by society as a bum, a no-good, degenerate alcoholic, here there flourished a spirit of creativity, full of life and spontaneity. My eyes filled with tears and my heart ached with the poignancy of this scene. Somehow, I knew Ralph had to be encouraged to keep drawing. Somehow, I believed in this newly discovered passion, the secret meaning of Ralph's existence awaited discovery.

And Ralph certainly did continue to draw. Over the next few weeks, anonymous gifts from our hospice staff began appearing outside his door. There were drawing pencils, a fine sketchpad, brushes, and watercolors. Ralph never questioned where these gifts came from. He just accepted them with equanimity, the same way he had accepted the fact that he had kidney cancer. He remained focused and drew his pictures with a hunger that seemed to consume him at times. While he taped a few more drawings to the wall he left others sitting in his notebook, not really needing to display his talent or receive praise for his creations. When I asked if he might like to put some of them in picture frames he looked confused and replied, "Why would I want to do that?"

Meanwhile, as Ralph continued to draw his physical condition began to improve. When he had outlived his prognosis by a month, we decided to recheck his blood tests. Sure enough, Ralph's kidney function was miraculously getting better, to the amazement of his oncologist. We had no explanation for this change other than the fact that Ralph's creative energy was so vibrant and so full in every moment that it seemed to be healing his physical body.

Before long, because he was spending so many hours each day drawing while hunched over with the catalog on his lap, Ralph began to experience some backaches. He decided he would like to have a special desk upon which to do his drawing, one with a top that would tilt up to support his sketchpad. The next time I came to Ralph's apartment, which for me was no longer a place filled with dread and foreboding, he showed me a page he had creased open in the middle of his catalog. There he had circled in red ink a picture of a piece of furniture entitled "Student Desk," which had a slanted top and a storage space underneath for all his art supplies. "This is it," Ralph told me proudly. "This is the desk I'm going to get as soon as I save enough money." The fact that it was a child's desk featured in a toy catalog didn't matter to Ralph at all. He had found a way to make his dream come true, and it would only cost him $35.00. He had been managing to save $5.00 each week from his pension check and within a few more weeks he would have enough money to send away for the desk.

Eventually Ralph was able to mail a money order to the toy company for his precious student desk. The catalog had specified a three to four week waiting period for shipments to be delivered. Ralph demonstrated infinite patience during this time, quietly awaiting the arrival of the desk as he continued to draw on top of the catalog. He tore out the picture of the desk and taped it on the wall next to his drawings where he could look up at it every now and then. The knowledge that the desk was on its way seemed to be enough for him as he remained totally content and happy with his life.

However, Ralph's next lab tests were somewhat concerning because his kidney function had worsened a little. But there was nothing more to be done for him and he seemed to be feeling well, so we simply waited with him as we hoped the student desk would come soon.

One Saturday morning a few weeks later I received a call from Ben, the neighbor and friend who looked after Ralph from time to time. He asked me to come and see Ralph because he was having some pain and "didn't look right." When I got to the little apartment I was surprised to see Ralph in bed, bent beneath his covers. This was the first time I had ever known him not to get up and get dressed. He told me his abdomen hurt and he felt too weak to walk, but he refused to go to the hospital or allow an IV to be started. With limited options available, I simply tried to make him comfortable and bought some Gatorade for him from a nearby convenience store, hoping that fluids and some mild pain medication would help him rally a little.

Shortly after I returned from the store we heard a knock on Ralph's door that turned out to be the mailman. He was delivering, what else? . . . the student desk. I helped carry the large, heavy box to Ralph's bedside, thrilled that I could be present for the unveiling of his long-awaited desk. Ralph's face glowed as he reached out his hand to touch the box and gave a long sigh of satisfaction.

"Should I open it for you?" I asked, hoping this would be just the inspiration Ralph needed to bounce back once again from this state of decline.

"No. I just want to look at it in the box for a while. After I rest a bit I'll open it."

The look on my face must have betrayed my mixed feelings of disappointment and concern over the fact that Ralph felt too ill to open his precious desk. He looked directly in my eyes and said, "Thank you for everything you've done. You've been most kind and I feel much better. You can go now. I'll be OK." His face, which was usually deeply creased and roughened from his years of hard living, was now soft and relaxed with a slight, beatific smile. I felt his compassion flow toward me as he tried to reassure and soothe my worry. I knew that he was right—it was time for me to leave. Ralph had always been a loner and he needed his solitude. So I squeezed his hand and walked out the door for what would be the last time. The hospice nurse arrived for a visit later in the day and reported that Ralph was finally free of pain and resting comfortably. But the next morning I received a call from Ben, telling me that when he went down to check on Ralph, he had found him in his bed, cold and lifeless. He did mention that Ralph's face bore a soft, peaceful smile and was still turned toward the box that held the student desk.

Our staff met that day to share our grief over the loss of Ralph, who had come to mean so much to each of us. His joy in the simplest of pleasures, his ability to be fully present in each moment, and his humble dedication to his creative talent had transformed every one of us who had gotten to know him. When we learned that no one had stepped forward to claim Ralph's remains, and that therefore his ashes were to be buried in a common paupers' grave, a staff member went to the crematorium and declared him to be a member of our "hospice family." We planned a small memorial for him and decided to bury his ashes near the river where he had always loved to fish.

At the last minute I stopped to tell Ben about the service in case he wanted to attend. To our surprise, twelve people who were all residents in his apartment building joined us to say farewell to Ralph. As we stood together in a circle surrounding the burial site, I looked around at the faces of his friends. There was an elderly couple, a young mother with two children in a stroller, a heavily made-up woman in a tight-fitting dress and high-heels, a teenaged boy wearing black leather with multiple piercings and a Mohawk haircut. Spontaneously, each person in the circle came forward to place a handful of dirt on the site where we buried the ashes and speak a few words about Ralph. They all called him "Pops" and told us special stories of their interactions with him. The teenaged boy shared that he had often come to Pops' apartment after school to wait for his mother to return from work. Once Pops had taken him fishing when he still had enough strength to get outside.

We were amazed to learn about this little family of diverse friends Ralph had accumulated during the time he lived in that apartment building. They each loved him just as we did, having been transformed by him in some way. That small funeral was the most profound memorial I have ever attended—simple, honest and totally spontaneous—just like Ralph, who cherished his last days on Earth as if he had found Paradise. Indeed . . . I believe he had.

THE SEEDS OF PARADISE

This intriguing story of Ralph, a man who owned almost nothing and yet seemed to possess everything, teaches us the next lesson: dwelling in the present moment is the key to Paradise. When he was left with only his existence in the present moment, Ralph was able to tap into his own artistic ability, something he had never before experienced. His earlier life as a vagabond had provided a type of training ground for him as he wandered from place to place without plans for the future or recognition of the past. But the breakdown of his physical body produced the stillness he required in order to see the creative visions within and manifest them on paper.

Viewing ourselves in present time, rather than the past or future, is a difficult task for our Western minds, But the dying are pushed to that perspective when the future is abruptly taken from them and this moment, here and now, becomes the only thing that still exists. To learn the wisdom of the dying, we are asked to study the art of dwelling in the present moment in order to further our spiritual growth and advance our consciousness in the world.

Balance in the Present Moment

The concept of present time is challenging for us to grasp because our minds have been trained to focus on either our memories of the past or our dreams of the future, both of which are fictional. The mind excels at rewriting the past and inventing the future, endlessly thinking and imagining; but the present moment just "is" and compels us to "be" rather than think. The present moment is actually the instant of transformation when "what will be" becomes "what was." Therefore, the present is suspended between past and future, a slender thread upon which we must balance. When we are not accustomed to bringing our awareness to the present moment it seems to be so fleeting that it cannot be comprehended. However, the practice of focusing on the present actually creates a sense of expansion in each moment, providing us with infinite opportunities for growth and creativity.

One paradox of the present moment that makes it so difficult to comprehend is that it is both perfectly full and perfectly empty at the same time. The present contains all of our unbound energy that has been freed from the knots and tangles of the past and is brimming with possibility. Yet the present moment is completely empty of thoughts, expectations, judgments, and emotions. Again, we must balance between fullness and emptiness as we attempt to live in each and every moment of the present. To be certain, this is a daunting task, and even the most highly enlightened teachers and gurus struggle to dwell always in the moment. But any attempt to remain in the present, no matter how feeble or brief, adds richness and depth to our living, opening the door to Paradise.

Learning to balance in the present, like all of the other spiritual lessons, is a process that requires a great deal of time. Therefore, patience is one of the qualities that must be cultivated on this path of development, though it seems to be a vanishing attribute in our society. However, genuine growth in consciousness is a process that cannot be rushed or streamlined. We must complete each and every step with dedication and integrity even as we acknowledge that there really is no goal and only this present moment matters. And from time to time, as we have seen in many of the stories of the dying, the present moment also allows for sudden transformation, changing everything at once. This, too, is a paradox that must be held and balanced along this path. The work of spiritual growth takes an infinite amount of time while transcendence occurs in an instant. Remember that paradise already exists—you are surrounded by and have unlimited access to paradise. Just open your eyes this moment and see what has always been and is already here right now.

Practice Mindfulness

"The most precious gift we can offer others is our presence.
When mindfulness embraces those we love,
they will bloom like flowers."

-Thich Nhat Hanh

In order to become aware of the present moment and enhance your ability to live there, you must retrain your mind and gain control over your thought processes. The practice of mindfulness is one of the training regimens you can implement to help discipline the mind. Mindfulness consists simply of focusing all of your attention and awareness on whatever exists for you in the present moment. In other words, any activity you are engaged in should fully occupy your thoughts during that activity. As you read this paragraph, for example, each word should fill your mind and command your total attention.

While this sounds like a simple concept, stop for a moment and consider how infrequently we are single-minded in our daily lives. Most of us practice multi-tasking in a variety of situations throughout the day. We check emails while we also talk on the phone or jot down reminders on our to-do list and straighten up our desk; or we cook something on the stove while we also wash a few dishes, watch a television program, and help our children with homework; or worst of all, we send text messages while we also maneuver our car through traffic, listen to the radio, and yell at other drivers. Our minds are amazing instruments that have the capacity to perform multiple functions at once, and we have maximized that ability in our fast-paced, ever-changing world. But the practice of mindfulness requires us to cease all our busyness, to slow down and truly contemplate a single moment in time.

Right now, wherever you are, you can practice stopping everything for just one second and focusing on only one thing. Perhaps this is the feel of paper under your fingers, the color of the wall next to you, the scent of perfume in the air, the sound of voices in the room. Notice how time seems to slow down just for that one second as you bring your full attention to an object in your awareness. There are many other practices for developing mindfulness that can be helpful as you seek to discipline your thoughts.

One significant benefit of the practice of mindful living is the richness it can add to relationships. To be fully present to another person, listening with your ears, mind and soul to every spoken word, is to grace that person with respect, honor, and love. One of our deepest desires is to be truly heard by others—to know that they have listened to us and comprehended our true nature. Mindful attention to those you love is a gift of tremendous importance that cannot be underestimated. This practice should also be extended to yourself as you carefully observe your own body for signs of health or illness, your thoughts for evidence of troublesome knots from the past, and your soul for intuition and guidance for your actions.

Express Gratitude

Another practice that can help you stay focused on the present moment is to intentionally experience gratitude for life. When you first begin to practice gratefulness, you should stop what you are doing at any given time and allow images to come to mind of the many things for which you are thankful. Again, this is a process that focuses your thoughts and serves to train the mind to maintain constant awareness of gratitude. Eventually, further along the spiritual path, thankfulness will simply flow from the heart in a continuous stream, manifesting in each and every moment. Gratitude must be cultivated over time and requires genuine spiritual effort, but when experienced in the fullness of the present moment it is another key to Paradise.

*   *   *

I once visited the home of a couple whose lives had been devastated by Alzheimer's disease. The husband, Joe, was nearing the end of a fifteen-year bout with this destructive illness and was confined to bed, unable to speak or communicate with his wife Doris. Our hospice staff had been requested to assist Doris in providing day-to-day care for Joe, to help her bathe him, change his clothing and linens, and turn him from side-to-side to avoid pressure ulcers on his skin. We had participated in the care of many patients with Alzheimer's, seeing firsthand the toll the disease exacted from family members and friends who served as caregivers. Many times we resorted to admitting those patients to nursing homes in order to save the health of their loved ones who became exhausted from providing the necessary care. But when Doris opened the door of their home to me on my first visit I noticed immediately how lovely she was and how a sense of exuberance and vitality seemed to emanate from her, which was not at all what I had expected. Their ranch-style home, situated on the edge of a forest in the foothills, was spotlessly clean and well ordered. Joe's hospital bed was in the living room facing glass doors that opened to the wooded backyard and allowed sunlight to fill the room with pleasant warmth.

Joe was deep in a coma and totally unresponsive to me as I examined him because he was in the terminal stage of his illness. He remained calm and peaceful throughout my visit. I was struck by the immaculate care he was receiving, clearly due to Doris's single-handed efforts. Tending a patient in such a comatose state requires constant attention and energy, and usually one person is overwhelmed by the task. When I sat down to talk with her I felt compelled to ask Doris, "How are you managing to provide such wonderful care to Joe all by yourself?" She smiled at me and responded, "I don't think of it as work. It's my privilege to be able to care for such a wonderful man and show him how much I love him. I'm grateful for every moment that I get to be with him." She went on to say that love and gratitude just seemed to flow out of her heart toward Joe in every moment, no matter what was happening. And she could feel him sending back to her, in his own way, mutual love and thankfulness. I told her I could

> *sense the energy of love in their home and it was deeply moving to*
> *me. Just then I glanced out the glass doors to see a buck deer with*
> *full antlers grazing contentedly in the backyard. "Oh, that's Joe's deer,"*
> *Doris explained. "He's been coming here every day for the past few*
> *years. When Joe was still able to be awake, watching that deer was the*
> *most important part of his day. He counted on it—and the deer never*
> *failed him. He has always come to our backyard, every single day." She*
> *then paused and with tears in her eyes added softly, "Now it's the most*
> *important part of MY day. I'm so lucky to have such a blessed life."*

*   *   *

What a gift it is to be grateful for every moment even while living with the consequences of a devastating disease like Alzheimer's. This is the essence of Paradise: taking each point of time as it comes, mindfully doing the work that is required, and fully expressing love and gratitude in every present moment.

Trust Providence

> *"Paradise—*
> *I see flowers*
> *from the cottage where I lie.*
> -Yaitsu—Death Poem 1807

Another aspect of the lesson of living in the present moment is the promise that you will have what you need in Paradise. When your energy is harnessed in present time, you are free to tap into the abundance of the Universe and will be provided with the experiences and resources you require in order to grow and thrive. In today's society the concept of abundance has become very popular, promising the potential of attracting to your life your "heart's desire," whether it is wealth, relationships, or power. The Internet and bookstores are full of courses, ebooks, and teleseminars teaching the process of attracting abundance to your life. However, the promise of paradise is that you will have what you *need* rather than what you *want*, and many disciples of the abundance philosophy have not managed to distinguish between those two ideas.

Frequently, we are so blinded by the things we want in life that we are unable to recognize what we really need. Many of us are consumed with desire and a sense of never having enough, and we fail to see the abundance surrounding us with exactly those things we actually require for our spiritual growth. True abundance comes to us in small ways and can go unnoticed if we are not fully attentive in the present moment. I worked with an elderly gentleman who was terrified of the idea of his coming death until he experienced a revelation. While seated at his kitchen table one day, he looked up at the mountainside visible from his window and saw an image of the face of Jesus silhouetted in a snowfield. The spring thaw had caused the snow to melt in such a way that it formed dark and light patches that truly did resemble a picture of Jesus. The man was so moved by this vision that he totally lost his fear of death, spending hours each day staring at the image on the mountain. He believed he was receiving a message from God and the Universe that all would be well. When the time came that he could no longer get out of bed, his wife placed his hospital bed in front of the living room window so he could continue to see that image. And as to be expected, the snowfield remained intact throughout the spring and did not finish melting until after his death. Truly, our needs are met in Paradise in ways that we could never anticipate or even imagine. When we recognize the beauty of this fact, those things that we want and desire seem shallow and insignificant in comparison.

When you truly exist in the present moment, there is no desire; therefore you are free to accept whatever is offered to you by life as a blessing. In the story of the Alzheimer's patient, Doris was blessed by caring for her terminally ill husband and dedicated to being of service to him in every moment. She experienced the daily visitation of the deer in the backyard as a sign of love and support from God and the Universe surrounding her. Here is evidence once again of the fundamental truth that spiritual growth arises from a focus on giving rather than receiving. When you enter each moment abundantly full, then you can freely give of your bounty to those around you and will ultimately take in everything you need without even striving to do so. If you live solely within the neediness conjured up by your ego, you may attract some of the things you want, but you will never be filled or satisfied by those things. Paradise consists of being fully present in every moment, freely sharing all that you have with others, and trusting in Divine Providence to fulfill your needs.

THE FRUITS OF PARADISE

Once you learn to live within the present moment, even if you only accomplish it occasionally, many benefits will begin to flow into your life, just as we have seen in the preceding stories. Again, these are the attributes of a spiritually growing being and they, in turn, will help lead you to even further growth and fulfillment.

Vibrancy

The word "vibrant" means pulsating with life, which describes the quality exuded by Doris when she was caring for her husband and by Ralph when he began drawing his pictures. When you successfully manage to dwell in present time you bring with you all of the energy that had previously been stuck in the past, tangled up in memories. The presence of this quality of vibrancy is readily apparent to others, bringing inspiration to them and enabling deeper connections to form. There is also the likelihood that physical health is enhanced by this vibrant energy as it provides the body with adequate resources to maintain healthy cell tissue and immune function. Ralph's condition improved for a surprising number of months and Doris was able to withstand the tremendous physical and emotional stress of being a caregiver without demonstrating any ill effects. Paradise, then, perfectly full of possibility, is really the life force that is fully present, vibrating with the Universe, waiting for you to take up residence there.

Serenity

Freedom from the anxiety of desire and want is another attribute attained from learning to live in the moment. In these stories, those who managed to find Paradise exhibited a quiet calmness that helped soothe fear and worry about the future. The gentleman who saw the face of Jesus on the mountainside was able to confront his death with serenity and acceptance once he relaxed into the present moment and focused his attention on the vision he was given. When you live in the now, there is no future to worry about and no past to mourn. The true gift of this serenity is that you no longer waste time and energy overanalyzing situations, imagining catastrophes and stressing about uncertainties.

Serenity is a quality that is visible in your behavior and appearance and that benefits everyone around you. Just one person emanating supreme calmness from within can single-handedly quiet an angry mob or soothe a group of frightened individuals. In an earlier story Nancy, who provided care to her brother-in-law Greg with a serene and loving presence, created a calm oasis in that angry household so that transformation could eventually occur. As we look toward finding solutions for the problems facing our world, serenity will surely be a necessary attribute for the leaders of change.

Creativity

When energy is released from the past and becomes available in the present moment, creativity flourishes, as demonstrated by Ralph who discovered his own hidden artistic talent at the end of his life. Ruby, the artist who lost her sight, was also able to tap into enhanced creativity as she faced declining health. Creativity springs from abundance, the presence of unlimited life force within and around us. However, moments of inspiration often arise from pain as suffering opens up the channels through which creativity flows. In this way, suffering plays a role in the manifestation of paradise within our lives. When you can embrace suffering without resentment and remain in the present moment, then you will have the energy necessary to create new ideas, solutions, art, and beauty. When abundant energy is available in present time you are free to respond instantaneously to changes and opportunities that arise, maximizing the benefits that are received. You can remain light and open, alert to everything surrounding you and attentive to others in every situation. Miracles and other extraordinary events occur only in the present moment and you must be capable of spontaneous creativity in order to fully appreciate them. At times you are called to act upon your intuition in order to set in motion the workings of transformation even though you cannot see the outcome or understand the purpose.

Momentum

The final "fruit" of dwelling in the present is momentum, a concept borrowed from the science of physics. The principle of momentum can be simply described as the tendency for an object in motion to remain in motion at the same speed, meaning that once something is moving, it can be difficult to stop. Of course, momentum could refer to movement toward either a positive or a negative goal. But regarding spiritual growth, momentum is motion toward greater awareness and higher consciousness. When you activate the present moment by bringing to it your focus and energy, you begin a cycle of movement within yourself that will have a tendency to continue. Thus, whatever action you begin in this moment is likely to carry over to the next moment and the next. When you send a ripple into the pooled energy of the Universe it will move ever and ever outward, impacting everything it touches. This is precisely the mechanism by which your small actions can have great impact on the planet. However, it is important that you respect the principle of momentum and act with your highest integrity, sending out only the ripples of your best effort for the greatest good. You must remember that momentum arising from negative impulses such as greed and fear also exists and impacts the Universe in a destructive manner.

THE VIEW FROM THE GARDEN

To discover Paradise, you must work to bring your awareness, whenever possible, into the present moment rather than focusing on the past or future. You will benefit from practices such as mindfulness and gratitude since this awareness does not come naturally to the mind. If you learn to trust that you will have whatever you need to assist you in your process of spiritual growth, you will open the door to increased creativity and serenity. Remember that you must find a balance between the past and the future in order to tap into the potential held in the present moment.

THE VIEW FROM THE GALAXY

When you ascend, once again, to the highest possible vantage point to observe the present moment, you can recognize that only this one moment in time actually exists. And within this one moment, everything is absolutely perfect—Paradise. Yaitsu wrote in his death poem that paradise is seeing flowers from the cottage where he lay dying. In a previous story Rita experienced a similar paradise as she gazed out of her window at the flowerbed planted for her by her loving son, Danny; Ralph's paradise was to draw the visions he saw in his head; and for Doris, paradise was providing care to her husband in his last days of life. All things come together, complete and whole, in this present moment of Heaven on Earth. You already possess everything you need for this one moment. There is no desire, fear or longing in the present, just perfect peace. Even if you are not yet able to dwell in this moment for an extended period, you can taste the sweet perfection of the present any time you stop, for just one second, and suspend yourself in the balance between past and future. This is the essence of paradise—stringing together moment after moment after moment of perfect emptiness and perfect fullness until you have an entire lifetime of wholeness and meaning, infused with the divine through and through.

WHAT REALLY MATTERS ABOUT PARADISE

Paradise is the space between past and future
where your potential becomes your path.
Dwell in the perfection of the Present Moment.

Lesson 5

Purpose: Manifest Your Highest Potential

*"My God, my God, for this
I was kept (this was the destiny
for which I was born.)"*

-Matthew 27:46

When we become adept at dwelling in the present moment with our energy fully available for spontaneous creativity, we will begin to explore the next lesson from the dying: "Manifest Your Highest Potential," which is the true Purpose of our existence in this lifetime. To discover the meaning and purpose of life has been a quest throughout the ages of man that continues to drive both spiritual and secular seekers today. Valuable information can be gleaned from the stories of the dying to help illuminate the answers to these questions.

The statement by Jesus upon the cross used here from the Book of Matthew is translated much differently in the Aramaic New Testament than in other versions derived from the Greek text that refer to Jesus questioning why God has forsaken Him. According to George Lamsa, a scholar of the Aramaic language and Middle Eastern culture, Greek translators probably misunderstood this remark because it is an idiom, having a cultural meaning that is not obvious from the exact words.[15] The idiom is translated in the parenthetic expression of the quotation, "This was the destiny for which I was born." Regardless of the translation used, it does seem clear that Jesus recognized, both before and during His dying on the cross, that He was fulfilling His destiny and manifesting His highest potential. The entire life of Jesus can be seen as leading up to this moment when His death redeemed all of mankind, untangling the knots of the past, embedding the concepts of love and forgiveness in human consciousness for all time.

As those seeking to grow in consciousness today, we ultimately must contemplate the purpose of our own lives and understand the driving force behind our existence. We feel a deep longing within to follow the correct path and fulfill our destiny. However, our concept of purpose and our definition of a meaningful life have gone somewhat astray as we have succumbed to the lure of accomplishment and acquisition that define a successful life in our contemporary society. To remember what really matters, we turn to the story of Ashley for an illustration of the purpose of life.

A VESSEL OF LOVE

From the moment I first heard the case of Ashley and her parents at our staff meeting, I dreaded my visit to their home. Ashley had been diagnosed with a rare progressive neuromuscular disease while she was still a toddler and had never been able to sit upright on her own or walk. With breathing and feeding difficulties and with her mental development arrested at the toddler stage, Ashley had been expected to live only a few years. Her parents kept her at home, determined to provide care for her until the end of her life. Now, eighteen years later, Ashley was still alive, against medical odds, and had become a new in-home patient of our hospice. At that time, I possessed a great deal of maternal anxiety and I worried constantly about the health and safety of my own children. Because of my difficulty managing my own fears of loss, I couldn't imagine how Ashley's parents coped with the pain of their daughter's illness and all the losses it brought to their lives. They would never see her play with friends, dress for a prom, graduate from high school, or marry her beloved. I didn't know if I could bear to share their anguish when I met with them or if I would fall apart with my own fear and despair.

My mood was somber as Dale and Joan showed me into their living room, for I had come prepared to encounter bitterness and resentment from them. So much had been taken from Ashley at such a young age. Certainly this was one of those instances when the unfairness of life was overwhelming and inexplicable. Therefore, I expected this family to need all the emotional and spiritual support our staff could offer. However, to my surprise, I found

Ashley's parents to be quite joyful and pleasant as they told me their story. Though their own lives had been dramatically altered by Ashley's need for round-the-clock care, they were totally accepting of this situation. They described how they alternated shifts, with Joan providing the bulk of the care during the day while Dale was away at his job. Dale covered the nighttime hours, getting up when needed for extra duties. The two of them had taken only a few days of vacation during the past eighteen years when friends and relatives filled in for them. I was astounded by their dedication and their total lack of resentment or disappointment. Surely this was not the life either of them had envisioned for themselves or for their daughter, yet they were completely at peace with the destiny that had befallen them. I couldn't fathom how Dale and Joan had reached this state of absolute acceptance and never-ending patience and I expressed to them my admiration.

When they brought me to Ashley's room I saw that the walls had been painted a sunny yellow and were stenciled with bright floral designs. A mobile comprised of characters from the Winnie the Pooh stories hung over her bed while dozens of colorful stuffed animals decorated the windowsill and shelves. Ashley was sleeping peacefully in her hospital bed with soft music playing on a stereo. She was dressed in a lacey white gown and her curly golden hair fell in ringlets around her face and across her pillow. With a slight smile on her lips, she looked like an angel, so beautiful and serene. My heart was touched to see the loving attention Ashley was receiving from Dale and Joan who clearly cherished her and their role as caregivers.

Though she was in a deep sleep, I spoke to Ashley before I began to do my exam, explaining who I was to reassure her that I would not hurt her and describing how I would listen to her heart and lungs. This was my usual practice with comatose patients who can still hear and process information and should always be treated with respect and gentleness.

After I completed my exam, including checking the tube that had been inserted into her stomach for feeding, I pulled the comforter back up over her arms and chest. Then Ashley opened her eyes, turned her head toward me with a wondrous smile and said, "I love you." Her eyes penetrated me and I felt an electric sensation run through me that I can only describe as pure, heavenly love. I was speechless, totally awestruck, as if in the presence of God. I stood there for a moment basking in the light that seemed to be vibrating around me and emanating from Ashley's face. Then I glanced at Dale and Joan, who were standing in the doorway, observing the entire scene. Their eyes glistened with tears and they smiled at me knowingly.

Instantly, I understood everything. Ashley, in her innocent and childlike nature, had become a pure vessel for the transmission of Divine love. Her parents had watched this blessing unfold many times as Ashley had touched other visitors with her loving energy and they understood that it was their privilege to have been chosen to care for her. Clearly, they too were constant recipients of this love. No wonder they were so joyful and so accepting of this outcome. For all that had been lost, so much more had been gained by the tragedy of Ashley's illness. They had been unable to describe this to me because there are no words for such an occurrence. They knew I would have to witness it and receive the blessing for myself.

While I have had many profound experiences during my work with hospice patients, never before or since have I felt so completely transformed by those three simple words, "I love you," the only three words Ashley was capable of speaking. For weeks following that encounter I could still feel the pulse of that Divine energy flowing through me as if I had been instantly transported back to that point in time. After years of studying spiritual concepts and principles, I had, for once, experienced the actual presence of the Divine in that single moment. And for all the complexities of religious history and the diversity of beliefs, dogmas, theologies and philosophies that dominate the sphere of spirituality, here it was, so simple and unassuming and utterly magnificent—the love of God, Heaven brought to Earth through the suspended life of a child. Ashley, manifesting her highest potential, was living a life of pure Purpose, as were her parents, turning upside down our contemporary notions of finding a path, following bliss, and searching for meaning. It remains for the rest of us to overcome our elaborate intellectualizations and tangled notions and convoluted concepts about our existence. Perhaps then we will finally see the uncomplicated answer to the most fundamental question: Why are we here?

THE SEEDS OF PURPOSE

Ashley's story beautifully introduces the concept that the search for the purpose of life can lead to an unexpected conclusion. We cling to the belief that there is a special path for us to follow that will include great accomplishments, a sense of satisfaction and an unequivocal contribution to the betterment of the world. There are classes and coaches available to help us search for this path and at times to change our course of direction to get on the right track. Our sense of fulfillment in life depends on discovering what we are supposed to be doing and then carrying that out. But Ashley's life followed a very different route. Suspended in her development, she could live only in the present moment, having no awareness of past or future. Within the present, free of thoughts, emotions, expectations and desires, her energy could be fully and spontaneously utilized to attain her highest potential. Take a closer look at some of the seeds of this concept.

Purpose Exists Within

Contrary to popular beliefs, purpose is not something that can be sought outside of oneself. There is no map for finding purpose and no outline for planning the events of life that will lead to the reason for existence. Purpose is also not a goal or a target that can be aimed for and measured. Purpose lies within us and has always been a part of us. Ashley's story demonstrates to us that thinking and planning are not necessary for finding our purpose, for she was capable of neither. In fact, excessive analysis and preparation may actually impede the discovery of purpose, since purpose emerges in the quiet spaces, the stillness which lies between our thoughts. From this perspective, every single life has a purpose and a reason for existence. There is no "wasted" energy in the Universe, no random or accidental or meaningless occurrence. However, there is also no predetermined destiny or fixed outcome to life, for whatever exists in the present moment is spontaneous and creative. The challenge of understanding and living a life of purpose is the difficult task of being still, quieting the thought processes, and allowing oneself to be suspended between the past and future.

The search for purpose in life goes hand-in-hand with the longing to discover a path toward tomorrow, as if there is a "yellow brick road" laid out to guide you to your destiny. However, the path of your life is actually created by you, one step at a time, from moment to moment. You are already on your path. You may not recognize it, however, because you are searching for a "superhighway" of destiny rather than a twisting, meandering road that only appears with each and every stride. Again, purpose and path are found within and already exist without seeking or searching.

Purpose Exists Only in the Present

The fallacy behind the search for life's purpose is that it usually projects you into the future. Purpose becomes something you will do or want to do someday. You become oblivious to what is here, inside, right now as you seek for something better or more significant or more fulfilling. But as long as you dwell in the future, you will not be capable of recognizing the purpose that resides within you right now.

Because of Ashley's illness and the tragic consequences it had upon her functioning, she could live only in the present and her parents were continually drawn to the present moment as well. The kind of care they were called to provide to Ashley required them to be available, alert and energized, always in the present, to deal with the uncertainties and sudden crises that go along with chronic, debilitating illness. In a similar way, Doris, who cared for her husband with end-stage Alzheimer's in a previous story, was kept constantly in present time, through her caregiving duties. Doris, like Ashley's parents Dale and Joan, was blessed by recognizing that, indeed, she was already living her purpose each and every day and needed no map or plan to discover why she is here.

In fact, it is interesting to note that Alzheimer's disease, while tragic and devastating, often has this paradoxical effect of trapping its victims and their caregivers in the present moment. The disease erases recent and short-term memory, negates the future, and causes the mind to replay an event as if it is continuously arising, perpetually new. Perhaps this is a small blessing within the tragedy of Alzheimer's. Consider this in the following story of a nursing home patient.

*   *   *

On my first day of work at a local nursing home, I visited individually with several of the patients, getting to know them and their medical histories. While I was talking with John in his room, another patient, Oscar, interrupted us by walking in and singing out, "Happy

Birthday!" He then gave John a big hug before moving on down the hallway. "Oh, Happy Birthday!" I exclaimed as well, shaking John's hand as he beamed with joy. A short while later, as I sat at the nurses' station writing my notes, I overheard Oscar wishing another patient, Marge, "Happy Birthday!" I remarked to the two nurses sitting near me at the desk, "It's so sweet that Oscar remembers the other patients' birthdays!" The two women just looked at one another and smiled, saying nothing to me. Two weeks later, though, when I sat down to talk with Oscar and he wished ME a Happy Birthday, I realized that these were the only two words he ever spoke. It seemed that Oscar was trapped perpetually in a state of celebration of birth and joyously reminded everyone of their special day over and over again. But the other residents of the nursing home didn't mind Oscar's repetitive behavior at all. In fact, not particularly aware of the calendar date or the passage of time, they embraced the idea that every day was their birthday, an occasion to be recognized and honored. In his own way Oscar created a festive and cheerful atmosphere in that nursing home where each person, including staff members, was made to feel special every day, even if for just one moment.

*   *   *

It could be said that Oscar was in a very simple manner living his purpose in that nursing home as he brought forward the best outcome he was capable of producing. Again, it is clear that living a life of purpose has nothing to do with one's intellectual prowess, education, or status. Purpose consists of living in the present moment at the highest level possible for the circumstances.

Being Rather than Seeking

*"Be yourself. Life is precious as it is. ...
There is no need to run, strive, search or struggle.
Just Be."*

-Thich Nhat Hanh

One of the qualities exhibited by both Ashley and Oscar is the simple capacity to "just be" who they were, through and through. Neither of them demonstrated any trace of pretentiousness, manipulation, or deceit. Neither of them strove to impress or achieve, master or improve, understand or obtain. Of course, the potential for those activities was missing for Ashley and Oscar because of the limitations of their brain function. But nonetheless, each of them was able to "be" exactly who they were in each moment in time. While we must struggle with minds that overanalyze and get stuck in the past or future and egos that desire recognition and control, it is important to remember the lesson of Ashley and Oscar. Being yourself in the moment is basic and simple, requiring only that you let go of other mental activities. In fact, you already are yourself; you don't have to do anything, seek anything, or struggle.

But this concept is immensely difficult for the rational mind to grasp since it lies outside the realm of thought. The human mind is comfortable in the past and the future because it can create images and stories with which to explain its own existence. Thus for the mind, purpose must be found in either the past or future and must consist of a rational or tangible goal. For the mind, purpose cannot be understood in the context of the present moment. To "just be" requires the quieting of the mind and the suspension of thinking, which paradoxically necessitates a certain amount of practice and training. However, you must remember that learning to "be" is not about achievement or accomplishment; it involves removing the obstacles that prevent you from seeing who you really are.

Purpose is Potential

"Sitting quietly, doing nothing;
spring comes,
and the grass grows by itself."

-Zen Proverb

In the previous lesson we learned that the present moment is full of potential, containing pure energy ready for action. Purpose consists of manifesting or activating this potential—bringing it to life. In the garden the flower seed contains all the potential of the flower with the energy necessary for growth and blossoming, through which its purpose is realized by becoming the most beautiful flower possible. This is a key concept, for achieving purpose does not equal perfection; to express your purpose is to be the best possible *under the given circumstances*. Ultimately, your flaws and imperfections are an important component of your purpose, your being.

Your limitations shape the eventual outcome, but do not prevent you from manifesting your best possible self. In fact, your shortcomings, your wounds and your illnesses, are necessary for the fulfillment of your unique potential. That is why both Ashley and Oscar can be described as living their purposes, and by incorporating all of their challenges, their best possible selves were evident in the present moment.

In other words, in the "garden of life" each individual is responsible for producing the best crop possible, given the limitations of soil, weather, and location of the plot of land. Your best crop will differ from that of all others, but will be a unique reflection of your individual identity. You are responsible for bringing the final product to life and for the integrity of your effort. But the ultimate outcome lies in the potential that already existed in the seeds of your garden, outside of your control. Ashley and Oscar had no control over the forces that limited the functioning of their brains; without mental obstacles to "just being" they were able to manifest their highest potential. Your work lies in consciously removing your mental obstacles so that you can "be" and manifest the highest potential within you.

When this highest potential is activated in your life, it will, of necessity, be a force for the greatest good for all of existence. If, in every moment, you manage to "just be" and activate the maximum capacity within you, then you will make wise choices, behave with integrity, and create the best possible path for your life as you proceed, step-by-step. Focusing upon your own highest potential in every moment, rather than trying to discover a perfect path for yourself to follow, will allow the strands of your life to fall in place to enable you to take the right action at the right time. From this perspective, this planet and the universe are calling upon you, not to just seek solutions to the problems we face, but to "just be" and manifest your highest potential. In this way the very answers you desire are contained within that potential. When you can live from that highest place you will bring to life the forces capable of untangling the threads and untying the knots not only of your own existence, but also of the planet.

Embracing the Mystery

Ultimately, the future remains a mystery for each of us and we must find a way to live with that fact. Bringing our attention to the present moment and to our highest potential still does not alleviate our anxiety and uncertainty about tomorrow. In addition, because we live in a hectic contemporary society rather than a secluded monastery, we are forced to make plans and to schedule our lives far in advance. We have to imagine and predict what might be taking place months from now in order to be prepared and organized, even though we have no way of knowing if our plans will come to pass or be totally interrupted along the way. At the same time, for the sake of our spiritual growth, we are being asked to dwell in the present and focus on our potential, which can surely seem impossible and pointless as well. It is no wonder that we suffer from stress-related disorders such as depression and anxiety; we are being pulled in opposite directions by powerful forces.

Once again, the solution to this dilemma lies in finding a balance. You can continue your patterns of planning and scheming for the future, but you must bring in a new focus and perspective: the present moment. When faced with a difficult decision that will impact the future, you must search out your highest potential and make the choice that will result in the greatest good. You must work tirelessly in the present to remove your obstacles of arrogance, resentment, selfishness, and self-pity in order to be free to make the best possible decisions and plans for yourself and for the entire planet. You must keep your highest and best possible self always in your awareness as you go through the activities of each day, never betraying or abandoning your purpose. You must recognize that fulfilling your purpose may not direct you toward one specific occupation, for there may be many types of work that allow you to manifest your potential. However, no matter which occupation you choose, you must give it your best and highest effort since the *quality* of your work is of utmost importance. And you must embrace fully the fact that the outcome of the purpose for your existence is unknown and mysterious to you until it actually unfolds. You must be able to live within the dynamic tension between knowing and not-knowing, applying yourself and letting go, caring deeply and being detached. This is the dance of mystery upon the razor's edge of life.

THE FRUITS OF PURPOSE

The spiritual growth that we have been discussing is a process that takes place in very small steps over a long period of time. As you begin to devote a small amount of your energy and attention to the present moment and discover your purpose within, you will gradually develop some spiritual skills that will assist you along the way. These "fruits" will ripen and nourish you as you struggle to find the balance in your life, and they will also help to alleviate some of your stress and anxiety as you proceed. Ultimately, you will come to recognize all of the previous lessons within the embrace of purpose: suffering, love, forgiveness, and paradise. As you grow, you will return to each of those tasks and continue your work, applying your new skills and moving to a deeper and broader perspective of each teaching. Truly, from this point on it will be clear to you that all of the seven lessons of the dying are intertwined and cannot be separated, though you must learn them one at a time. Finding your purpose is the key to comprehending the profound meaning of these lessons, and growing the following "fruits" is essential for bringing the lessons to life.

Diligence

The definition of "diligence" is "attentive or heedful care," but the root word from Latin is *diligere*, which means "to love or esteem." To be diligent, then, is to provide care that springs from love, instilled with purpose. When you act with diligence, you consider all possibilities, leave no stone unturned, and persevere until the task is completed. This quality was evident in the care provided by Ashley's parents and by Doris who tended to her husband stricken with Alzheimer's disease. All three of those caregivers put aside their own concerns about time, accomplishment, enjoyment, and relaxation in order to give impeccable service to the ones they loved. You, too, are asked to be diligent in all your work, devoting yourself with pure intention, in the present moment, undistracted by external forces. While every task you perform deserves your diligence, you should choose your activities wisely so that your attentive care is not squandered on some wayward or destructive project. For this reason you must cultivate discernment, as well, so that you can direct your actions toward those things that really matter and not be distracted by the superficial.

However, it is also true that every small act you undertake is equally important to the larger tasks of your life. Whether you are stirring the soup, smoothing a blanket, tying a shoe, or opening a door, each small action deserves your full attention and diligence. There is a saying in the Buddhist tradition that the work of spiritual growth requires one only to "chop wood, carry water," emphasizing that transformation lies in the mundane tasks of daily life and how diligently they are completed. In our garden metaphor, you are asked to "plant seeds, pull weeds" as you tend to your growth and develop the full potential of the seeds you have been given. This is not glamorous or distinguished work; in fact, it requires getting dirty and grimy and going unnoticed, without recognition. But this labor forms the basis of all spiritual transformation and must be given a priority in your life.

When you are anxious about the future or lost in planning and anticipation, you must constantly return your thoughts to your garden within and perform your daily tasks with diligence. You must pull up the weeds of resentment and fear that tangle and strangle healthy roots and trim away the expired and outmoded parts of yourself to allow new growth. On a physical level this parable reminds you also to return to the necessary small tasks of life whenever you feel overwhelmed. Wash a dish, sweep the floor, or clean the mirror in order to return to the present moment. Diligence in all things will ultimately lead you to the spiritual growth you desire.

Accountability

Once you begin to apply yourself with diligence to the purposeful tasks of the present moment, you will naturally move toward accountability, taking responsibility for your actions. When you hold yourself accountable you pay attention to the results of your behavior, acknowledging both successes and failures, and facing the consequences when the outcome is less than intended. Sadly, accountability is another character trait that is noticeably absent in our society. Many of our most serious societal issues have arisen because of a lack of accountability at some level or another. Faulty automobile braking systems, the subprime mortgage crisis, collapsed mineral mines, contaminated eggs, leaking oil wells, and tainted over-the-counter medications are all examples of disastrous outcomes that could have been prevented had appropriate diligence and accountability been practiced at every stage of operation from start to finish. Demonstrating our individual lack of accountability, courtroom dockets are overflowing with personal injury lawsuits as people attempt to establish blame and seek compensation for the unfortunate events of life.

However, from a spiritual point of view it is most important that you scrutinize your own behavior, motives, and weaknesses. You must take responsibility for every word you speak, every task you perform, and every outcome you create. Only through accountability can you grow toward manifesting your highest potential and fulfilling your purpose. You must always be aware of and honest about your shortcomings if you are going to be the best possible person. Living your purpose requires self-knowledge before you act, diligence during your tasks, accountability for the results of your efforts, and authenticity through every moment. In addition, fulfilling a higher spiritual purpose necessitates taking responsibility for the impact of your actions on all of creation, not just your small sphere of influence. Again, as another paradox of advancing consciousness, you are called to bear in mind the good of the whole while focusing your attention on the details of your own day-to-day life.

Once when I was visiting a hospice patient just hours before his death, he opened his eyes, lifted his head from the pillow, and said to me in a commanding voice, "Don't say it if you don't mean it." Those words became etched in my mind from that point on, and many times I have been reminded of that wise advice when I have found myself speaking without first evaluating the accuracy and the intention of my words. The struggle to be always authentic, diligent and accountable is a work in progress that continues for a lifetime. But the struggle itself yields rewards as you move closer and closer toward manifesting your highest potential.

Clarity

One of the benefits of expressing your potential with diligence and accountability is the presence of greater clarity in your life. Clarity is a rich word filled with layers of meaning and metaphor, a perfect descriptor for the balanced state of purpose in the present moment. The word depicts a quality of being luminous and bright, like a cloudless sky, as well as being transparent and serene like a deep pool of still water. Innocence and purity are additional images conveyed by the word clarity, along with being plain and unmistakable. Applying each of these definitions to the story of Ashley and her pure transmission of Divine love, it is apparent that she exemplified clarity in every possible image and interpretation of the word. Her face and smile were luminous while an aura of serenity surrounded her. She was also totally innocent and plain in her offering of love and her words were unmistakable in their meaning. As we have already determined, Ashley achieved this state of clarity by simply manifesting her highest potential in the present moment.

Embracing all the nuances of clarity can help create an elegant image for contemplation or meditation. Picture a cloudless sky as you seek to quiet your thoughts; imagine a deep pool of still water as you calm your emotions; recognize the luminous and unmistakable presence of the Divine within yourself and within everyone and everything you encounter. Clarity of the mind can lead to better decisions and more accurate judgment in any situation. Clarity of the emotions can foster more authentic functioning and more honest communication in relationships. Clarity of the soul can lead directly back to this present moment and its simple and unpretentious potential for creativity.

Achieving genuine clarity requires a great deal of work in the garden to remove the weeds of resentment that flourish there and to cut away the old decaying stalks of misperceptions that can no longer be supported. It is a lifelong task that cannot be rushed or skipped, that thrives on patience and diligence, and requires an attitude of giving rather than receiving. As with each of the previous lessons you are asked to focus on that which you bring forth in the world, your offering to life, rather than concentrating on the gifts you inherit. So, too, the path of your life is not a thoroughfare blazed across the wilderness for you to follow, but is determined by the flagstones of potential you lay out before yourself one moment at a time. The greater your clarity, the better you will see the potential of the present and the more easily you will remain there, resulting in an even deeper sense of fulfillment.

Contentment

"Ever since happiness heard your name,
it has been running through the streets
trying to find you."

-Hafiz

As the final gift of purpose, you eventually reach a state of contentment in which you are filled with the light of potential energy. The word "contentment" is derived from the Latin word *continere*, meaning "to hold in or contain." Then, to be content means to contain or be filled with enough; to be without lack or want. This quality describes many of the characters we have met in previous stories: Ralph, the vagabond who discovered his artistic talent; Ruby, the sculptress who lost her sight; Doris, Dale, and Joan, the caregivers who were grateful for the opportunity to provide total care for their loved ones. Each of these people was content in the moment with the circumstances of life. Each expressed gratitude for life and each concentrated on giving and bringing forth the best possible outcome for the circumstances.

Being in a state of contentment really requires accepting the fact that what you have is exactly what you need; that is, there is nothing missing, nothing more you require. Most people are far from achieving this state and maintain long lists of goals, wants, aspirations, and wishes. In an attempt to advance your own spiritual growth you might be tempted to focus on denying your desires or eliminating them. However, contentment cannot be manufactured or forced by disciplined behavior; it arises spontaneously as a product of living in the present moment, manifesting your highest potential. So your efforts are best directed toward balancing in the present rather than trying to free yourself from desire. The sensation of insufficiency will subside some day along this path as purpose fills the gaps and contentment ensues. Each person must grow at a unique pace and in the proper season, just as gardens grow. Seeking to accelerate your tempo or leap ahead to higher levels is like picking fruit before it ripens or cutting flowers before they bloom.

Patience is required along with a focus on this present moment and the sufficiency of current circumstances. Some spiritual practitioners attempt to rid themselves of all desire, believing it is a sign of weakness or failure. But desire really represents a longing to further manifest your potential and is a normal aspect of the spiritual growth process. When you experience desire in the moment, allow it to remain as you concentrate on compassion for your own development. Focus on the fact that desire is simply a sign of your unrecognized potential rather than focusing on the object of the desire. Sharpen your senses so you can see the potential more clearly, feel its energy, and hear its calling. Then you will gradually learn to respond, to manifest your potential, and be filled with purpose. Rest assured that contentment will find you, no matter where you are.

The View from the Garden

Your purpose already exists within you and consists of manifesting your highest potential in every moment. Your task is to balance in the present moment, quieting your thoughts that prevent you from just being who you really are. When you activate your highest potential it will be a force for the good and lead ultimately to solutions for the problems facing the planet. The outcome of the purpose for your existence is a mystery until it unfolds. You must work diligently on your spiritual tasks of "planting seeds, pulling weeds" and hold yourself accountable for your actions. In this way you will eventually achieve clarity and contentment in your life.

The View from the Galaxy

In a spiritual sense, the purpose of all life is to be the bridge between Heaven and Earth, Garden, and Galaxy. You are a manifestation of God, the Divine, on this planet and in the Universe. By giving life to or animating the Divine potential within you, you provide God with a physical form through which to act. When you are pure in your manifestation of this potential you can become a direct conduit of Divine presence, just as Ashley was in the story that began this chapter. The goal of manifesting your full potential contains within it an image of bringing together all the diverse parts of yourself: uniting the unconscious, the Shadow, with that which is conscious, and joining your undeveloped and weak aspects to your greatest gifts. There is no other reason for the existence of the Universe other than to be a diverse, pulsating, evolving manifestation of God. And you are simply and amazingly a part of that manifestation. Aside from your goals and insecurities and desires and opinions and seeking and striving, you are only here to BE that which you already ARE.

The highest and best part of you knows that this is true, but it cannot be fathomed by your mind. Stop for one moment. Consider the cloudless sky, the still deep water, the luminous light from a loved one's eyes. You are here only for this and all of this is here only for you. Breathe. Set out to give life to all the potential that vibrates within you.

But take time and take care. Let it unfold. Allow contentment to find you. It will happen in an unmistakable instant, the perfect moment, the infinite Present.

WHAT REALLY MATTERS ABOUT PURPOSE

Purpose unfolds continuously in the Present moment,
creating your path one step at a time.
Manifest your highest potential by being who you already are.

LESSON 6

Surrender: LET GO OF EXPECTATIONS

"O my Father, into thy hands
I commit my Spirit."

-Luke 23:46

Once we have learned that the purpose for our existence is to manifest our highest potential, our task becomes to "Let Go of Expectations" for our lives, or Surrender. The concept of surrendering is an important component of the teachings of Christianity, Buddhism, Hinduism, and Islam, as well as an essential element in the Alcoholics Anonymous program and in yoga and bodywork practices. In each of these cases, the word "surrender" generally means to give up power or to let go of resistance. In the stories of the dying, surrender also plays an important role as individuals confront the end of life and seek greater understanding of their suffering.

When Jesus spoke the above words on the cross, He was nearing the end of His own ordeal of suffering and was entrusting His spirit, that which would remain after the death of his physical body, to the hands of God. In this simple prayer, Jesus teaches that spiritual matters belong in the realm of the Divine and He trusts God to manage the outcome of His existence. The fact that He refers to the "hands" of God creates an image of safety and nurturance, a place to rest and relax, free from worry, while being held in love.

The word surrender is derived from *rendre*, which means, "to give back." In this sense, Jesus surrendered or gave back His spirit to That which had given life to Him. We are asked, as well, to give back the life force we have received, placing it in the hands of the Divine and trusting the wisdom of the Divine, no matter the outcome. The fact that we are returning this life force implies that it wasn't really ours to begin with. Therefore we should give up our expectations willingly, as beautifully illustrated in the following story of Andy.

The Face of the Divine

When I first learned that Andy was being admitted to our hospice service, I placed a phone call to a medical school classmate of mine who was by then a cancer specialist. Andy's diagnosis of advanced squamous cell carcinoma of the face was a condition I had never seen before and I wanted some expert advice before I went to visit him for the first time. My friend told me that this is a disease that is often brought on by years of smoking, alcohol abuse, neglect, and self-loathing. Warning me that he has found these patients to be the most difficult to care for in his practice, he described the insurmountable issues they experience: severe pain, isolation, and low self-esteem due to the disfigurement of the face caused by the spreading cancer. Before we hung up he added, "About 25% of these patients take their own lives during the course of treatment, so be prepared for that."

All of my fears were confirmed by that phone call. I was going to be taking on a huge challenge with Andy as a patient and I wasn't sure I had enough experience or confidence to be his doctor. In addition, I was still healing from my father's suicide and wondered if I could withstand the potential of losing a patient to this same fate. However, I had to acknowledge that this is what had unfolded for Andy, our staff, and for me. For some reason we were being brought together and I needed to be open and ready for all possibilities.

As I stood on Andy's front step, knocking on his door for the first of many visits, I noticed an odd combination of decorations visible on the outside of the house. There were Christmas lights hanging from the eaves and a cardboard Halloween jack-o'-lantern in the window. This was notable for the fact that it was the month of May and tulips were blooming in a planter near the steps. But this confusing array was not really surprising, for time, seasons, and holidays are often awry in a home where someone is dying. I could surmise that Andy's condition had taken a turn for the worse sometime around the previous November, exhausting his energy and interest in tending to superficial things such as holiday decorations.

I swallowed my fears and entered the house as Andy called out to me that the door was open. It took a moment for my eyes to adjust to the darkness inside the living room where the window shades had been pulled tightly closed. When I could see more clearly, I found Andy sitting in a rocking chair near the door with an unfolded square of four-inch gauze carefully taped over the left side of his face. He greeted me warmly and offered a handshake, apologizing for the darkness that was necessary because the cancer had invaded his eyes and caused light to be excruciatingly painful for him. As I gathered myself and found a seat on the couch facing Andy, I noticed that the TV set was tuned to CNN with the volume at a low murmur. My mind was racing, trying to decide what questions to ask and how to begin, when Andy spoke first, "So tell me about your work with hospice—how did you get interested in it? What do you like best about this type of medicine?" Just like that, Andy and I were chatting away as if we were two old friends discussing life, our children, and the presidential election that was coming up in the fall.

Suddenly I recognized that I felt completely comfortable and at home sitting here with a man whom I had expected to be my most difficult patient. Andy had completely disarmed me with his pleasant and outgoing nature and his concern for my comfort and wellbeing rather than his own. I learned that he was divorced and had two pre-adolescent children who lived with their mother but stayed with him two nights a week. He was an adoring and proud father, directing me to a bulletin board in the kitchen where I could see pictures of the children, their artwork, and special notes they had written to him. I was moved by his deep and visible love for his offspring and imagined the gentle and supportive care he must provide to them.

Returning to the living room, I realized that Andy and I had not yet discussed his medical condition: the cancer that had ravaged his appearance. It had destroyed his nose, left cheek, and part of his mouth, leaving him with a gaping hole in the middle of his face. Somehow, I thought, Andy had purposely directed the conversation to other easier topics until we both felt safe with one another and could handle the discomfort of this subject. In a straightforward manner Andy told me the history of his cancer, the failed surgeries and treatments, and the eventual realization that nothing was going to stop the progression of this deadly disease. He had lost the ability to chew and was limited to a liquid diet, though swallowing even a milkshake was becoming difficult. His cancer doctors expected him to live only four to six months, but he was determined, despite the pain and horror of his disfigurement, to live as many days as he could manage. Seeing his children grow and providing them with as much love as possible was the motivation for his every action and the justification for carrying on despite his suffering.

I was stunned by Andy's selflessness and calm determination. There was not a trace of bitterness in his heart as he coped with his devastating condition and painstakingly cleaned his wound in front of the mirror every day, struggled to take in enough liquid calories to keep from wasting away, and balanced his pain medications to remain totally lucid and alert for his children. In his presence that day, I felt I had encountered a rare individual, a spiritual master of sorts who devoted his entire existence to the good of others. However, I would eventually learn that the previous decades of Andy's life had been quite a different story.

By his description, Andy had been an angry, self-destructive man in his earlier years, drinking too much, too often, and ignoring his general health. His out-of-control behavior had led to the demise of his marriage while his children were still very young. Deep inside, he despised himself and his life and cared little about anything or anyone. But sometime after being diagnosed with cancer, everything changed. As his face became increasingly disfigured he spent more and more time alone, eventually holing up inside his house and never going out in public. With hour after hour of time available to him for contemplation he was forced to look at himself and life in general. Watching the news on CNN became one of his favorite pastimes, and as he took in the stories of tragedies and struggles around the world, something inside of him began to shift. He saw himself as part of a larger picture, a piece of the puzzle of life. He recognized that suffering of one form or another came to every person, of every race and ethnicity, in every part of the world. His tragedy was just a fraction of the tragedy of the whole planet. But at the same time, he witnessed all the beautiful ways in which suffering was overcome by people helping one another, reaching out and sharing from whatever portion they had been given in order to enrich others. Over time, Andy had been profoundly changed by both his own suffering and his immersion in the suffering of the planet. He awakened from those years of contemplation with the knowledge that giving his love to his children for however many days he could hang on, was the only thing that really mattered for his life.

Andy managed to keep himself alive for another year after becoming our patient, and I had the privilege of visiting him on many occasions. Always ready to discuss current events, such as the recent crash of an airliner in the East, or the then-current conflict in Africa, or the competition for gold medals in the Olympics, Andy enabled me to see both the tragic and glorious moments of our existence through his eyes that were sharpened and enlightened by suffering. Each time we met I marveled at his equanimity, his total acceptance of his life circumstances. Though he fought with every breath to remain alive, he was fully at peace with the knowledge that death could come at any moment. He never questioned why he had this disease but understood that this is just the path his life had taken. His ability to surrender to the events of life as they unfolded created an aura of calm wisdom and clarity about him that was profoundly tangible to those in his presence. Andy was my teacher and guide during that year as I learned about suffering, purpose, paradise, and surrender through his life and death.

One day near the end of Andy's life, I helped him change the gauze that covered the wound on his face since his arms and hands were now too weak to perform that task. As I cleaned away some drainage and dead skin from the side of his face he said, "I'm so sorry that you have to look at my ugliness." Bursting into tears, I hugged him as I cried, "Oh my God, Andy. You are the most beautiful person I've ever seen." He whispered, "Thank you," as tears silently trickled down his right cheek.

In the end, I recognized that Andy, in his simple and straightforward manner, had allowed me to look at myself in the mirror, to have the courage to behold my own ugliness. And he had taught me how to live with my wounded and damaged parts, slowly incorporating them into my awareness, gradually increasing my compassion toward myself and letting go of my expectations for my life. In Andy's face I could see the truth that life, no matter how it unfolds, is perfect in its own mysterious and fascinating way; and being awake enough to witness that unfolding is all that really matters.

THE SEEDS OF SURRENDER

Through Andy's touching story we see surrender in action and learn of the paradox presented by this lesson. In Andy's case, it was necessary to let go of every expectation, for he had no assurances that a future would exist for him. Yet simultaneously he gave every ounce of his energy to living each moment, being present in his greatest possible capacity and animating the spiritual energy within. We are asked to live our highest potential even while we hold no attachments to the outcome or possible accomplishments of that potential. This is indeed a delicate balance we must achieve, requiring skillful management of the mind and the ego, for our natural tendency is to look ahead and imagine what is to follow. When we first begin working diligently to manifest our highest potential, dreams of the future are often woven into the process and must be carefully sorted out and unraveled. This is one of the pitfalls along the path of spiritual growth that requires patience and time to master as we return over and over again to the simple and basic directive: let go of expectations. The following "seeds" of surrender help to further elucidate this difficult lesson.

Surrender to Mystery

In the previous chapter we learned that a challenging aspect of purpose is the mystery it imparts to life: "You must be able to live within the dynamic tension between knowing and not-knowing, applying yourself and letting go, caring deeply and being detached. This is the dance of mystery upon the razor's edge of life." While we desire to know the reasons why things happen and a logical explanation for our existence, the truth is that life is a mystery and certain answers cannot be known. During the course of his illness it was necessary for Andy to come to terms with this fact, or he might have expended his precious energy searching for solutions to unanswerable questions. He could have been led astray, seeking a path out of the mystery, but instead he committed to staying within the unknown and manifesting his potential without understanding the answers. Andy exemplified the deeper aspect of embracing the mystery of life by giving himself to it wholeheartedly and releasing all attempts to control the future.

The mind and ego desperately resist the notion of giving up control and foster inaccurate beliefs that have taken hold in our contemporary world, such as "The mind can control the Universe." The truth is that the only universe the unenlightened mind has the possibility of controlling is the tiny world inside its own head. And honestly, for most of us, the mind performs even that task poorly. Our society struggles with addictions, unhealthy lifestyle patterns, and negative emotional behavior, none of which the mind has successfully overcome. Our thoughts do have an influence upon our attitude and can either poison our efforts to grow or support them, but in the final analysis thoughts alone cannot create growth or lead to spiritual awakening. The mind can provide assistance to the process of spiritual growth through study, advancement of knowledge, and contemplation of the mystery. But ultimately, the greatest contribution of the mind toward the manifestation of highest potential is to let go and be still, removing obstacles that obscure the presence of the Divine.

In Andy's case, surrendering to the inevitability of his disease was necessary in order for him to begin living more fully as a spiritual being. At that point he began dancing on the razor's edge and dwelling in the mystery, as he threw everything he had into keeping his physical body alive from moment to moment and manifesting love for his children and all of mankind. He wasted not one particle of his energy on regret or resentment or blame and he looked no further into the future than the moment confronting him. As he carried through each day, suspended in this state of divine purpose between past and future, his presence had a profound effect on everyone who connected with him. Andy manifested vibrancy and clarity with every living breath, though he knew nothing of spiritual teachings and religious dogma. He was simply and purely his highest self, radiating divine love and acceptance for all of life. In the end, Andy's willingness to embrace the mystery of life with unquestioning determination helped him take the next step toward spiritual growth, which is to accept the results, no matter how life unfolds.

Surrender the Outcome

In our current society nearly every system that governs daily life has become outcome-oriented. From corporations to government agencies, schools, healthcare facilities, banks, small businesses, factories, and insurance companies, everyone who is engaged in production of any sort is concerned with measuring the outcome of activity. While it is expedient in business to use outcome data to analyze efficiency and determine next steps, focusing solely on results can lead your spiritual efforts down a frustrating path. Your purpose, or manifesting your highest potential, is driven from within by the presence of Spirit. That manifestation is the only true motivation for your existence. When you allow yourself to be driven by other impulses, you fall into a confusing and disappointing tangle of unmet expectations. I learned this lesson from two different patients, Marcus and Kathy, who were each moved to practice good behaviors in their lives, but for the wrong reasons.

*   *   *

Marcus had just learned that he was suffering from terminal cancer when he was admitted to our service. Because the disease was advanced and had spread throughout his body, there was no hope for remission and his prognosis was grim. Marcus wept with bitterness during my visit, pounding his fists with anger and frustration. When he was calm enough to talk a little about his history, he revealed that he had been very religious all of his life, carefully following the doctrine of his church since boyhood. He told me he had believed that if he did everything that was expected of him he would avoid being punished by God. In fact that belief had been the primary motivation for his religious faith. Now, upon learning that he would soon die of a dread disease, Marcus felt betrayed by God, his church, and the spiritual teachers who had led him down this road. "There were so many times I forced myself to choose the 'right' path or the 'good' behavior when my heart wanted to do something else," he cried. "I never enjoyed anything. I turned away from every pleasure, and I thought God would have no reason to punish me." Marcus believed that his illness was a penance from God, but he could not understand why, since his behavior had always been impeccable. His confusion and disillusionment caused him deep pain during his final days of life that required a great deal of work to resolve.

*   *   *

Like Marcus, Kathy had received a shocking diagnosis of terminal cancer after experiencing symptoms of illness for only a short time. She also was not a candidate for treatment because of the advanced stage of her disease. Her wrath was directed at the medical profession, for she had followed every recommendation she had ever encountered for preventive health care. Eating a strict vegetarian diet, exercising daily for many years, and having regular checkups and screening exams, she had rigorously followed a plan for healthy living that she believed would result in a long life, free of illness. That she was now dying of pancreatic cancer was devastating to her and she felt cheated by her medical advisors and life itself. "I did everything right!" she ranted, "This was not supposed to happen to ME!" Her bitterness and rage were directed toward everyone around her because she couldn't identify exactly who to blame for her condition. While Kathy, unlike Marcus, had never belonged to a church, she had followed her own doctrine for "right living" with a religious zeal, believing she would be rewarded in the end. She, too, spent her last days mired in deep disappointment and regret.

*   *   *

In each of these tragic stories, the dying patient is a victim of a misguided belief that life operates on a "punish and reward" system. Seeking an outcome of reward rather than punishment, both of them conformed their life choices and behaviors to an idealized doctrine of "right" and "good" behavior that was directed by others, not by the wisdom of their own hearts. And both of them suffered horrible disillusionment when the outcome was different than they had expected. Belief in a rational, "cause and effect" explanation for life was the initial misdirected step for Marcus and Kathy. From that belief rose the negative emotions of fear and greed, that is, fear of punishment and suffering and greed for rewards and comfort. These powerful emotions are both directed toward the future and both concerned exclusively with the *results* of their efforts rather than on the quality of each effort in the present moment. Because they focused so thoroughly on the desired outcome and they believed so strongly that they could manipulate and create that outcome, Marcus and Kathy both fell drastically into depression and despair when life took a different turn.

As difficult as it may seem, you are called to suspend your rational notions of how the world operates and embrace instead the mystery of life. You are asked to devote yourself to your highest potential simply because that is the impulse that is arising within you in each and every moment. Surrendering requires that you let go of thoughts that carry you to the dream world of tomorrow and, instead remind yourself that you know nothing of the future. For the future cannot be known and should not be known. Though you deeply desire to see what lies ahead in order to ease your fears and worries, it is possible that premature knowledge of the future could destroy your present existence. Whenever you use "outcome measures" to make predictions for your own future, in an attempt to manipulate the results, you play with the fire of false expectations and failed hopes.

This is the essence of Surrender: abiding in the knowledge that life, as the bridge between Heaven and Earth, is meant to be lived in the present moment—educated and informed by the past, aware of potential for the future—but free of attachments to either. The outcome, of course, is the delectable mystery whose unfolding you patiently await while balancing on the razor's edge.

Clear the Clutter

In order to carry out this challenging task of surrender, letting go of your expectations, it is necessary to do a great deal of inner work to clear a space for something new to arise, like pulling weeds from the garden. Part of what must be cleared from your heart and mind are the resentments and grievances you hold from the past. You must revisit the task of forgiveness to remove those old, debilitating memories and create clarity within. This process, repeated over and over again, gradually clears away the refuse of your previous life that distracts you from seeing the present moment. In the story that began this chapter, Andy, because of the isolation imposed by his disfiguring illness, spent months and months in solitary contemplation. During that time he cleared out many of the weeds of his past disappointments and misery and became much more attuned to the suffering of mankind. Manifesting new awareness or consciousness requires this creation of inner space to accommodate an even larger perspective of life. But you must be willing to let go of the past and relinquish any perceived power or entitlement that you gain from your wounds. Many of us have used our past history of injury and pain to manipulate power or sympathy from others, playing the role of perpetual victim. This behavior, along with resentment, must be identified as destructive and have its roots cleared away from the interior self. Forgiveness must be enacted toward others, yourself, life, and God before you can continue further on the path to spiritual growth.

In addition, you must also purge yourself of old beliefs that have been outgrown and now stifle your development. Many of these beliefs have been deeply ingrained and will have to be searched out and identified before they can be cleared away. Both Marcus and Kathy had beliefs that limited their ability to function without expectations. Often, as was true for those two individuals, our beliefs arise from positive intentions and actually represent "the good" in their essence. But it is the attachment of those beliefs to fear or greed or other negative emotions that cause them to be destructive. Your actions should be inspired by the movement of the Divine within and informed by your beliefs and training, but not dictated by those beliefs or training. It is necessary to clear away old ideas in order to make space for the newness that is constantly arising within.

Just as old ideas or resentments from the past can hinder your manifestation in the present moment, clinging to expectations for the future can also obscure the view of what really matters. Expectations that arise from insecurities, such as fear and greed, trap you in a feeling of dissatisfaction with the present as you impatiently focus on the future. Part of your work of clearing the inner clutter is to remove those limiting expectations, allowing openness to unfold instead. The degree to which you are willing to surrender the past and let go of expectations for the future determines the speed with which you manifest new spiritual growth. But it is a process that takes time and repetition, so once again patience and compassion are necessary as you tend your spiritual garden.

Active Surrender

While the word "surrender," when defined as giving up, seems to imply passivity or inaction, surrendering from a spiritual perspective is actually an active process that requires diligence and consistency. In fact, to surrender your past and future is a task that must be carried out in each and every moment with a positive intention toward letting go. Every moment arises with a new challenge to stay committed to the highest potential and eliminate all distractions in order to balance in the middle. While this process might seem overwhelming in the beginning, eventually it will occur spontaneously, for surrendering is a crucial aspect of manifesting your highest potential. Those two capacities, living with purpose and letting go of expectations, are intertwined and will grow and develop together over time.

The philosophy of Zen Buddhism teaches the concept of the "don't-know mind," which helps counteract over-thinking. Each time a thought arises, the student is advised to repeat, "I don't know" in order to emphasize the limitations of the mind and the mystery that exists in the Universe. It is impossible for the "don't-know mind" to have attachments or expectations because those require knowledge and thought. Zen disciples are taught that the "don't-know mind" leads to enlightenment because it is a reflection of emptiness and exists before thought. For our purposes, "don't-know mind" can help you let go of expectations for the future. Because you simply don't know what will happen, it is futile to worry or create unrealistic dreams. Instead, enjoy the task itself, relishing each step of the process and each component of the work. Enjoy your own effort and focus. Be motivated to do the project simply because it is the right thing to do right now.

Then when the project is completed, be willing to let go of it. Adopt a "don't-know mind" as you reject both excitement over the possibility that others will applaud your work and anxiety that some might offer criticism of your efforts. Try to stay balanced in between those two states: pleased that you have done your best work, but calm and content with not knowing what will come next. If you can successfully function in this manner, you will free yourself from a great deal of stress and worry. By keeping your energy and focus in the present moment you will enhance your creativity and your ability to move on to the next project or task; and you will avoid having to deal with feelings of disappointment and failure that arise when you derive your motivation from the future. Over and over you must choose to let go of the future in order to truly be alive and vibrant in the present.

THE FRUITS OF SURRENDER

When you begin to stabilize in the present moment, manifesting your highest potential and letting go of expectations, some positive character traits will be strengthened as a result. As we have seen, the previous lessons are all intertwined with the task of surrender and require continued focus and effort, particularly the actions of love and forgiveness. Because the lessons are really inseparable, learning them becomes a cyclical process, constantly revisiting each stage with new wisdom and a deeper perspective. By learning to surrender you can practice forgiveness and genuine love in a much more profound manner. In addition, the following "fruits" of mastering the art of surrender will be beneficial in the perpetual recycling that leads to spiraling growth.

Equanimity

One of the benefits of releasing expectations is the experience of a calm and even mind: equanimity. By focusing on the present and letting go of the future, you are freed from the constant vacillations of the mind between fear and anticipation, depression and exuberance. This quality allows you to tolerate stressful situations without getting lost in emotion and projecting yourself into the future or getting trapped in the misery of the past. Equanimity is a vital character trait in a troubled world, for calm consideration of the issues of the present moment is the only path to resolution. When the mind is still, possibilities open up and space is cleared for creativity to flourish. Once again, the image evoked by the concept of equanimity is that of balancing on a thin wire between the dangerous pitfalls of past and future. It is also necessary to avoid the traps of fear and greed as answers are sought to difficult problems, because those states will only lead to a twisted and wayward path that will likely cause even more suffering. The even mind is comfortable with not knowing and open to allow new ideas to flourish.

Adaptability

The next benefit of letting go, which follows naturally after achieving equanimity, is to become more adaptable. By releasing expectations, you create room internally for new growth and unanticipated developments. To adapt means to modify according to changing circumstances, an ability necessary when living in the moment. Focusing on the future creates rigid and narrow boundaries that restrict opportunities for change and obscure the recognition of those opportunities. Holding tightly to a desired and expected outcome can prevent necessary shifts in behavior that can lead to transformation. For both Marcus and Kathy, attachment to the expectation that their health would never suffer because of the good life they had lived became the source of misery and bitterness when a terminal illness was diagnosed. Each of them lacked the ability to adapt to a new circumstance that might have helped them transform at the end of life. Andy, however, was able to tolerate his declining health and adapt a new perspective on life and new behaviors because he had learned to surrender. Adaptability enables fluidity in the moment, freedom to move quickly from one situation to another and openness to react accordingly. This quality is essential in order for deeper growth and transformation to occur.

Harmony

Harmony is derived from the Greek word *harmos*, which originally meant a joint or fastening. Later the word *harmonia* was used to describe a joining together of parts in a pleasing manner. This is a lovely depiction of the state of harmony, in which there is internal calm and tranquility generated by the orderly connection of diverse components. Harmonious music results when various notes are joined together into pleasing chords and melodies. Spiritual harmony is created within when intention is united with potential in the present moment. Surrender is necessary for this harmony to manifest because attachments and expectations are disrupters of harmony. In some ways your very existence gives birth to a harmonious connection as you are the link between Heaven and Earth, and you also are the potential that hovers between past and future: diverse parts joined together in a pleasing manner. When you are able to practice surrender on a regular basis, you will develop an inner harmony that will resonate from you, extending peacefulness all around. Harmony also requires the act of clearing space to create an opening in which it can flourish. For example, it is the empty space inside the body of the violin that allows the reverberation of harmonious music from the instrument. A violin cannot fulfill its purpose without being empty inside. So, too, you must intentionally maintain internal clarity and openness by releasing old resentments and limiting beliefs in order to manifest harmony and your ultimate purpose.

Because of the internal work he had already completed and his ability to surrender, Andy's presence radiated a sense of harmony to everyone who visited him. In a similar manner, if we would hope to generate peace on our planet or begin to solve the issues of environmental disruption that face us, we must first achieve internal harmony as individuals. This will require practicing surrender and "don't-know mind" even as we search for solutions that might seem contradictory. However, it is often true that the most important discoveries occur when we are not even looking for them.

Synchronicity

Synchronicity is a word coined by psychologist Carl Jung in the 1950s to describe what he called "meaningful coincidences." These might be simple everyday occurrences, such as finding a coupon in your mailbox for the very product you were planning to buy that day, or suddenly recalling a long-forgotten friend and then running into that person later the same day. When these experiences happen, it suggests that somehow stars are aligning in the heavens or unseen forces are pulling together disparate events and creating a harmonious flow. But whatever the source, such incidents can be powerful reminders of the mystery of life.

Once when I was participating in a small group discussion in the home of a friend, a woman began sharing with us her heartfelt desire for peace throughout the world. At the very moment she described her dream of ending war, we looked up to see three white doves fluttering outside the window. The symbolism of that occurrence was powerful and moving to each person present in the room as we witnessed Nature's validation of the woman's quest for peace. When we move forward having clarified our intentions and let go of our expectations, harmonious events and even miracles can occur. The following is another story of synchronicity that occurred during my work in hospice.

* * *

I was once hastily loading medical supplies and my purse into my car as I prepared for a drive to a neighboring town to meet with a patient's husband. This man was extremely angry and hostile and had created a major disturbance at the nursing home where his wife was receiving care. I was quite angry myself because this was just the most recent of many upsets this man had caused and our entire staff was weary of his abusive behavior. I had started the day in a bad mood already and was primed to have a heated argument with him when we met. However, as I slammed shut the driver-side door of my car, a small notebook fell out of my purse onto the floor and landed open to a torn page somewhere in the middle of the book. The words written there caught my eye as I picked it up. The page was titled "The Lovingkindness Blessing," a prayer for compassion or "Metta," which is taught in some Buddhist traditions. I had copied it into this notebook several years earlier when a speaker at a conference had recited it during her workshop, but I had forgotten about it until that moment in the car. The blessing read:

May you be at peace.
May your heart be open.
May you know the beauty of your own true nature.
May you be healed.
May you be a source of healing for this world.

I recognized that this prayer was exactly what I needed that morning, and I began to recite those words over and over again as I drove. I spoke the blessing for myself and for the man I was going to meet until I felt perfectly calm and serene internally. Free of my own resentment and blame, I was able to recognize that his hostility was arising from his pain and grief. With renewed compassion rather than uncontrollable anger, I could connect with his feelings harmoniously and help him cope better with his own suffering. From that day on there were no further episodes of rage from the man as he sat peacefully with his beloved wife during her remaining days.

*   *   *

In one brief moment of carelessness a seemingly insignificant act of synchronicity occurred: a notebook fell open to a special page, gently reminding me to surrender to a purpose greater than my understanding and greater than my sense of pride. When I was able to let go of my need to be in control, my need to be right, and my expectations of how people should behave, the knots of this tangled situation began to work themselves out. Connections became possible and harmony was the result. In this same manner, you are asked to do difficult work as you put your effort into manifesting your highest potential, clearing space within and letting go of all your expectations. But the true marvel of it all, the secret that you don't know, is that you will have whatever you need to fulfill your tasks and sometimes it will come to you in amazing ways. To step into the flow of harmony and synchronicity, you must let go and let go and let go, continually surrendering to what is greater than you.

THE VIEW FROM THE GARDEN

You must suspend your rational notions of how the world operates and accept that life is a mystery, and therefore certain answers cannot be known. The act of surrender requires you to live from your highest potential while you simultaneously release your attempts to control the future and accept the results of your actions, no matter how they unfold. To accomplish this it will be necessary to revisit forgiveness as you clear away your internal clutter of past disappointments and resentments. You must also let go of expectations for the future and limiting beliefs, making a space for something new to unfold. In this way you will achieve harmony and open the possibility for synchronicity to occur. Adopting a "don't-know mind" will help you achieve equanimity and adaptability so that you can better manage the unanticipated developments of life.

THE VIEW FROM THE GALAXY

From a heavenly perspective, when you ascend to the highest realm you can imagine, to surrender is actually to become One with the Divine, to conform to the heavenly rhythm of all life. When plants grow in your garden, even while struggling to push through the soil and to sprout leaves and scatter seeds, they conform to the rhythm of the seasons and surrender to the elements, becoming one with all of Nature. When a small stream empties into a large river, it conforms to the flow of the river, surrendering its water and its separateness. In this process, the water of the stream unites with the ultimate Source of all water, becoming One again, cycling on and on to bring life to the planet.

When you surrender, you ultimately give back the life force you were originally given, returning it to the Source for the greater good of all as you tune yourself to the music of the Divine. In this way, harmony resonates throughout the Universe and within the holy space inside you.

Surrendering to what is greater, you will flow with the rhythm of creation, finding just what is needed for growth at just the right time. The life force will continually ripple through you as you diligently work to release the knots and tangles that obstruct the flow. The purpose of your existence will be revealed to be the uniting of all your disparate parts into one harmonious whole, including the subconscious Shadow that lurks below the surface of your awareness. Once you manage to bring together every particle of your potential, you will vibrate with the rhythm of the Divine, suspended between past and future in the paradise of the present moment. Surrendering to what is greater than you is the key to understanding all of the lessons of life and death.

WHAT REALLY MATTERS ABOUT SURRENDER

Surrender is conforming your path with the rhythm
of the Divine.
Let go of expectations for the outcome of your efforts.

LESSON 7

Impermanence: FACE YOUR FEAR

"It is fulfilled."

-John 19:30

The final lesson to be learned from the dying is to "Face Your Fear" by embracing the concept of Impermanence. This teaching represents both the culmination and the convergence of all the other lessons. Having begun this journey by embracing the challenge of suffering, we have practiced the tasks of love and forgiveness, bringing us to discover our purpose within each present moment and the necessity of surrender. Finally, we then come to the ultimate spiritual challenge, which is to confront our own mortality, seeking to free ourselves of the fears that cloud our consciousness.

These three words, "It is fulfilled," represent according to the Gospel of John the final statement of Jesus upon the cross, just before He "gave up His breath." The word "fulfill" is rich with meaning and symbolism, indicating in one instance "to bring to an end," but also meaning "to make full" and "to develop one's full potential." Jesus' death on the cross signified the end of His physical existence and the full manifestation of His purpose in this life. Having completed all that had been laid before Him on His earthly path, He surrendered the breath of life, giving it back to the Source from which He came, and transcended His broken physical body.

In this final lesson we are asked to learn that everything in our existence is impermanent: nothing will last. Death is interwoven in every moment of life. Facing our fear of ultimate destruction we must learn to balance that fear with inspiration and continue to live fully in every present moment. To accomplish this we must keep death always within our sights, continually unearthing our deepest fears and untangling the imperfections that cloud our vision. The following story tells of Lorraine, a remarkable woman who lived her life fully from this perspective.

IN THE PRESENCE OF A YOGI

I had been excited to meet Lorraine, a new patient on our hospice service since I first heard about her from the admitting nurse. She was a woman in her seventies who was suffering from metastatic breast cancer, which was a fairly common diagnosis among our patients. However, everything I had been told about Lorraine indicated that she was not at all an ordinary person. When the nurse tried to describe her to me, she kept running out of words and could say only, "She's amazing. She's fascinating." So I knew I would need to meet this woman myself in order discover her true nature.

On the morning of my first visit, I found the front door to Lorraine's apartment slightly ajar and could hear lovely music wafting from somewhere inside. There was a note attached to the door that said, "Come on upstairs!" I found Lorraine waiting for me in a huge sumptuous room that served as both a bedroom and a study. She was propped up in bed, wearing a red silk kimono, surrounded by brocade pillows in a variety of patterns and colors. Immediately I noticed the luminous glow that surrounded Lorraine and the lovely smile on her delicate face. As I studied her features I realized that I would never have guessed her age by her appearance. Her skin was clear and free of wrinkles, her eyes shiny and piercing in their gaze, and her laughter as light and melodic as that of a child.

Next to the bed was a small Asian table that held a silver tray with a porcelain teapot and two cups. "Please, take off your coat and sit down for a moment," Lorraine invited as she gestured toward an overstuffed armchair a few feet from her bed. As I sank into the comfy chair I became aware of how rushed and frantic I had been feeling all morning. Lorraine's cheerful presence and the beauty of the room seemed to draw me into a state of relaxation and calmness. As I sipped peppermint tea from a hand-painted cup, I realized that Lorraine was as eager to learn more about me as I was interested in her story. We traded questions back and forth in a lively conversation that made time stand still, as I forgot about all my other commitments for the day.

Lorraine was, among many other things, a writer and poet who had traveled much of the world in her younger days. Her room was filled with treasures and keepsakes she had gathered during her journeys, each one special to her for a specific reason. She had stories to tell about every item in the room and I could have listened to them for hours. Everything about Lorraine was rich and deep with character and meaning. Her room, her conversation, her life and her spirit, were filled with joy and sorrow, celebration and pain. I had never in my life met anyone like Lorraine.

During that visit I learned that Lorraine now confined herself to this one room, no longer having the strength to go downstairs. The lower level of her apartment was occupied at night by one of her children or grandchildren, who took turns staying with her in order to provide her care. She had been sick for several years but had not slowed her pace of living until the past few months when she began feeling very tired. She had continued to write poetry and stories even from her bed until her hands became too weak to hold the pen and paper. When she talked about having to give up her writing, she looked away with a trace of sadness, but only for a fleeting moment. Her attitude toward her illness and physical decline was one of fascination. She was observing herself, her body, mind and emotions, as if she were a scientist conducting a study. Each day held something new to discover and she found all of it delightful.

I was totally enchanted with Lorraine, and when she asked me to return the next week, I jumped at the chance to spend more time in her presence. It was clear that she had a great deal of knowledge to share and I wanted to learn everything I could from her. On subsequent visits we discussed the craft of writing, which interested me because I was a fledgling writer at the time. I had been struggling with an inability to finish my pieces, always feeling dissatisfied and that something was left undone. Each time I sat down and reread a paragraph I felt a need to add to it or start over again. This was frustrating to me since I had a notebook full of beginnings, but no endings for any of my writings. Lorraine listened patiently as I described my difficulties and then reached over and patted my hand consolingly. "You're not ready to be finished yet," she stated. In response to my puzzled expression she added, "When a piece is finished you'll know it. You're just not there yet. You have to learn to be patient." Of course, that wasn't the answer I was hoping for, wanting to find a quick and easy shortcut to finishing all my partial writings. But I recognized the wisdom of her words and knew she came by that wisdom through years of experience.

Eventually, Lorraine began to reveal to me that her peace of mind and joie de vivre arose from deep spiritual beliefs she had practiced much of her adult life. She had studied many religions, but rather than follow one of them exclusively, she had created her own practice of meditation, contemplation, and breathing exercises. This practice brought her tremendous calmness in the midst of her suffering and acceptance of the idea of her death. She expressed no fear or dread when we discussed the approaching end of her life, only fascination with the mystery that would unfold in the days ahead. Death was just another journey and she loved to travel. She looked forward to experiencing the unknown and trusted that everything would be fine, just as it should be. I had never before had such a frank and comfortable conversation about death with a patient and I continued to marvel at Lorraine and her astounding composure.

In order to be prepared for the future, I needed to have a discussion with Lorraine about her preferences for her final days of life. Up to that point in time, she had not required any medications for pain, but I wanted to plan ahead for the possibility that pain might become a significant issue in the coming weeks. Lorraine's cancer had metastasized to her bones and from my experience with other patients I knew that this could cause severe physical distress. However, Lorraine expressed an unwillingness to take any medication for pain because she felt it would cloud her consciousness and interfere with her ability to meditate. In my opinion, severe pain might also interfere with her meditation practice and I wanted her to agree that an appropriate medication could be administered if she seemed to be suffering intensely. Lorraine still refused to grant this permission, which deeply concerned me. I would be forced to follow her wishes, but I really believed that she was being naïve. In my opinion Lorraine didn't realize the extreme nature of cancer pain and might be left in a desperate situation if there was no medication available in the house for her caregivers to administer in an emergency. Lorraine just smiled at me with compassion, understanding that I cared about her wellbeing, and reassured me that she was very familiar with cancer pain—she had been living with it and managing well for months.

Of course, I hadn't recognized that she was already in pain because she never complained. But that was how Lorraine approached everything in her life, with equanimity and openness, excited to experience all of the ups and downs of existence. However, I was still afraid to acquiesce to her wishes, and so I made one last appeal to her: "What if the pain becomes unbearable, more than you can even imagine? What will you do then?"

With her pervasive patience Lorraine smiled again and said, "Well, if the pain becomes that bad, then I will know it is finished. I will know that it's time for me to pass on to the next realm, whatever that might be."

She was so serene and self-assured that I had to give up my argument. As she wished, the circumstances of her passing would unfold and we would all cope with whatever arose during her last days. But I was not at all convinced that things would go well. Lorraine may have planning that she would be able to leave this earth on a moment's notice whenever she was ready, but I had never seen anyone die this type of conscious death and I did not really believe it was possible.

On subsequent visits with Lorraine, she began talking to me in more detail about her meditation practice. I learned that she regularly experienced a state she referred to as "oneness with God," during which she could see the Divine in everything and feel her separateness dissolving away. This profound experience gave rise to her calm acceptance of life and death and her courage in the face of the unknown. Over the years she had done a great deal of work searching out her wounded parts, shining light on her own shadow, and developing harmony within. Her internal work of integrating her body, mind, heart, and soul had resulted in the radiant light and beauty that surrounded her.

During a later visit, Lorraine handed me one of her favorite books, a leather-bound edition of The Autobiography of a Yogi, *about the life of Indian guru Paramahansa Yogananda. I knew this book had been an inspiration for her own spiritual practice and I assumed she was offering to loan it to me. But she pressed it into my hands stating, "I want you to keep it. I don't need it anymore." I wondered if someone from her family might like to have this beautiful book as a keepsake, but Lorraine insisted that it was meant for me. It is a gift I still cherish these years later.*

That day would turn out to be my last encounter with Lorraine. Within a week she announced to her family that it was time for her to go and called them together to say goodbye. Her pain had escalated as I had feared, but she managed to cope without medication, just as she had predicted. A few hours later Lorraine lapsed into the state of active dying, still bearing her beautiful smile and radiant face. From time to time she opened her eyes and spoke to her family, expressing her love and gratitude. Then she would return to the mysterious state that is between worlds where she seemed to be resting peacefully. Finally, she opened her eyes for the last time and reached out to those surrounding her bed. With pure exhilaration and joy she spoke her last words, offering comfort and reassurance to those in her presence, "Oh, it's wonderful here! It's so beautiful!" Resting her head on the pillow again, Lorraine took her last breaths and slipped away, never losing her smile or her serene countenance. After her years of practice in entering an elevated state of consciousness, Lorraine had indeed been able to die when she knew her life was finished, just as she had told me.

Meeting Lorraine and learning from her wisdom had a profound effect on me. She taught me to be more confident in helping other patients address spiritual issues and more certain that life is a spiritual journey on a physical plane. Moreover, she helped ease my own doubts and brought me face-to-face with the idea of my own death, finally aligning my hidden fears with my highest beliefs. I now understand that I must patiently wait until "it is finished," allowing everything to unfold and manifest in its own time, neither pushing nor pulling, but just balancing and breathing in the present moment, spreading Light into the darkest corners of my being. Living a life fulfilled, as Lorraine did, spreads ripples of transformation throughout the Universe, making anything and everything possible.

THE SEEDS OF IMPERMANENCE

Lorraine's inspiring story introduces us to the concept of Impermanence and the effect of living a life with conscious awareness and surrender. Lorraine approached every aspect of her life with fearlessness because she had already accepted that nothing is permanent and had given up all expectations for the future. From this open perspective she was able to dwell in the present and enjoy everything that came to her, maximizing the potential of each moment of her life. Her understanding of the concept of "finishing" was that we will recognize it when we get there, so there is no reason to worry or struggle or seek for the future. Just keep filling up each moment, which paradoxically leads eventually to emptiness, and when the end arrives, embrace it wholeheartedly. We learned from Lorraine that it was her many years of spiritual practice that helped her achieve this place of equanimity. This is a reminder that patience and effort are necessary for growth to occur. But the path, no matter how long and twisting and precarious, is also full of joy along the way, for paradise dwells in every moment and every moment dwells in paradise. However, on our beginner's journey through life, there are some important aspects of impermanence to take into consideration as we study this lesson.

Impermanence is Essential

Even with minimal awareness of our surroundings on this planet we can recognize that everything eventually comes to an end. Starting with our traumatic exit from the watery warmth of the womb, to the final gasping breath of life, we are confronted every day of our existence with the reality that nothing lasts forever. Although this is one of our painful disappointments with life, it is one we somehow never quite adjust to and never quite remember. So it arises as a complete shock to us when a relationship breaks up or our car breaks down or our health falls apart. Somehow we don't really learn how to handle these situations, no matter how many times we go through them. Perhaps, that's because we excel at hiding the truth from ourselves. We have mastered the art of breathing life into illusion and parading it in front of ourselves as if it is the truth. But soon enough, the illusion collapses like a punctured balloon and we are left exposed once again to the pain and disappointment of life's impermanence, crying out "Why me? This wasn't supposed to happen to me!"

But there is a secret to our earthly existence that must be told: impermanence is *essential*, meaning it is both fundamental to and necessary for all of life. Impermanence is the doorway through which change arrives—change that brings with it growth and transformation. Without impermanence, stagnation would result, a quagmire of lifeless sameness that would swallow up everything in its path. Life is change; life is growth; life is joy and pain; *Life is Death*. We have already observed that our gardens must die in the winter to make room for the rejuvenation that arrives with spring. Trees must lose their leaves in the fall, crumbling edifices must be torn down to build new sturdy structures, obsolete beliefs must give way to breakthrough knowledge, failing systems must be replaced with modern functional technology. Without change life stands still and meaning is ultimately lost.

Yet universally, it is within our nature to fear change. Suspicious of the unknown, we resist and fight against newness, doubting that anything positive could result from the process of change. But the impermanence of everything around us exists to challenge our rigid foundations and push us toward the boundaries of possibility and potential. In order to continue growing in our lives, we must not only accept change; we must *embrace* impermanence.

The Spiritual Crisis of Impermanence

When we do succeed at becoming more conscious and more awake to our surroundings, we will inevitably be confronted with the reality of our own impermanence. Acknowledging our mortality and facing it straight on initially causes confusion and turmoil on the spiritual journey. Some fall into the trap of believing that the pursuit of a spiritual path will guarantee immortality, falsely bargaining with God to trade devotion for deathlessness in the physical realm. This is another illusion designed to conceal the truth of impermanence, but it always fails in the end. Those who succumb to this misconception and don't manage to grow beyond it during their lifetime experience bitter disappointment at the time of their death.

The truth is that the physical body must die, regardless of all efforts and hopes to the contrary. Remember that in spite of her lifelong spiritual devotion, Lorraine still developed cancer. Her spiritual practice helped her accept and manage her illness with grace, but did not guarantee her perfect health. Accepting this truth requires courage and honesty but ultimately leads to peacefulness and equanimity as demonstrated by Lorraine. When we overcome fear of death, there is nothing else to fear.

The point should be emphasized that your motivation to work toward spiritual growth must be nothing more than manifesting your highest potential. If your intentions for spiritual advancement are totally pure, the only focus of your effort will be on the possibility of the present moment and giving life to that possibility. But it is likely that many of your steps leading to this growth will become contaminated with false expectations, such as avoiding suffering, prolonging life, attaining success, garnering power, or maintaining control. It is important to diligently scrutinize every aspect of your spiritual efforts to detect these misdirected and hidden motives. Recall Lorraine, who through years of practice had managed to free herself of many of these common snares and achieve clarity and total sincerity in her spiritual life. You must remember first that everything is impermanent: suffering, life, success, power, and control. You keep starting over at the beginning in order to reeducate the parts of your consciousness that tell you otherwise.

The path of spiritual growth is not meant to be straight and direct. Turbulence and confusion are necessary and helpful on the journey in order to engage your creativity and foster your adaptability. Falling into traps helps you recognize their existence. Following an erroneous fork in the road teaches you how to find your way back on course. Descending into chaos points out the knots and tangles that still need to be straightened. Though confronting your mortality may cause panic and fear to arise, it also allows you to practice the art of restoring balance, breathing yourself back to equanimity. The more you train yourself to remain calm, the better you can cope with life's difficulties and with the moment of death, as Lorraine demonstrated.

Focus on the "Little Deaths"

Since impermanence is an intrinsic characteristic of everything in existence, life is really a series of small opportunities to rehearse the process of dying. In a sense, every breath represents a "little death" and can be used as training ground in the work to accept impermanence. Each complete breath, consisting of an inhalation and an exhalation, enacts the balance between fullness and emptiness, which is a characteristic of the present moment. The end of exhalation, when the lungs are completely empty, resembles the moment of death when the breath is "given up." The practice of breathing deeply while focusing on each individual breath allows you to experience over and over again that instant when the lungs are empty and to rehearse remaining utterly calm without grasping for the next inhalation. A similar breathing exercise Lorraine had used for many years enabled her to cope with severe pain at the end of her life. Confronting your immortality and practicing your little deaths can help you be prepared for any difficulty that may unfold for you in the future. The simple act of breathing in and out holds for you a profound learning opportunity on this path of spiritual growth as it anchors you to the present moment and recreates your entire lifespan from birth to death in a single instant.

Our breath, like our death, also connects us with all of life on this planet. We share the air we breathe with every life form, inhaling and exhaling the same molecules and atoms from earth's atmosphere across time and distance. This fundamental process is the primary act of life and, as such, is sacred to our existence. Breathing is also one of the methods by which the body removes waste products and toxins, purifying itself in every moment. In a spiritual sense you can utilize the breath to help you open within and create space by clearing away the waste and toxic weeds that cloud your vision and strangle new growth in your garden. It is an exquisite perfection that breathing, an involuntary function that is a requirement for your very existence, is the simple, sacred act that links you to all of creation and that purifies your body, mind, and spirit, portraying your birth and death in every present moment. In the final analysis, breathing is the only practice necessary for attaining awareness and advancing consciousness; and it is the one practice you cannot fail to perform while you are alive. Take heart, then, that you have been created to grow and advance and learn. You have been woven through every cell and fiber of your being with this potential. Inevitably, you cannot avoid this outcome, though your diligence and focused intention will certainly enhance the process to ease fear and anxiety along the journey.

Unite Fear with Inspiration

Just as our bodies are programmed for the act of breathing, our brains are "wired" to experience fear. This primitive emotion exists for our protection from imminent danger and connects the mind and body through the powerful firing of the sympathetic nervous system. Our fear response can be lifesaving when we are in a perilous situation, such as a near-collision with another car, stepping too close to the edge of a cliff, or being chased by a lion. However, it is a quality of daily life in modern society that fear has become a habitual state of mind along with the accompanying over-functioning of the sympathetic nervous system. This has occurred because fear, which ideally should operate only in present time, is being projected into the future and applied to every unknown situation.

Being misinformed by traumatic, unhealed memories of the past, we perceive the future as a threat and are trapped in a perpetual experience of dread and anxiety. But all fears have at their foundation the fear of death. Ultimately, our own impermanence is our greatest concern in this life, though we may not recognize it for the many disguises behind which it hides. Escaping this cycle of fear requires us to increase our awareness, clear away debilitating memories, and open the mind to new inspiration.

The origin of the word inspiration is the Latin verb *spirare*, meaning "to breathe." Inspiration can be defined as the act of breathing in, and also as "the action of moving the mind or emotions." Your inspirations breathe new life and ideas into the mind, opening the door for change to occur. Inspiration arises from your divine potential, lying within each moment, awaiting the intention that will bring it to reality. The impetus to develop a practice and grow spiritually is an inspiration that has been built into your being and calls to you at various times throughout life. However, inspiration, the touch of the divine in your life, is overshadowed by the fear that is the mark of your human existence on this planet. To rise above the paralysis created by fear you must connect your fear to your inspiration by breathing in and out, with focus and intention, in the present moment. Through the breath you can unite Heaven and Earth, fulfilling your divine purpose and accepting the impermanence of this existence.

Death as a Teacher

We have to learn to die in every moment
in order to be fully alive.

-Thich Nhat Hanh

When we learn to surrender to the reality of our impermanence and recognize that it contains the potential for our spiritual growth, death can emerge as a teacher in the classroom of life. If we keep a calm eye always on our death, never allowing the fickle mind to pretend it doesn't exist, it is then that death can become a lens through which we view all of life with the potential to change our perception of everything. The dying have taught us that each moment of our existence becomes significant when we realize that it could be the last moment of life. In the shadow of death, even the tiniest spark of light is precious and does not go unnoticed. When death is knocking at the door the last bite of a peach is the sweetest and most succulent of all; the final touch of a lover is silk upon the skin; the closing note of a melody is the breath of an angel; the red and pink hue of the sunset is the brushstroke of a master; the swaying of a hollyhock blossom in the breeze is the genius of creation. Only against the backdrop of death, can life fully manifest in all its diversity, chaos, and imperfect elegance. Only within the rhythm of a single breath can life be witnessed and embodied on this planet. Only within the present moment can life unfold and unravel, revealing step by step the mysterious path of this existence.

THE FRUTIS OF IMPERMANENCE

To utilize death as your teacher you must keep your focus on the impermanence of the present moment, live as though this moment might be your last, and give yourself fully to every experience and inspiration that life provides. This lesson is difficult to practice and will require great diligence and effort. It will be necessary to return, repeatedly, to the present moment and remember that nothing is permanent, until fear begins to fade and doubt gradually diminishes. Many other benefits will result as you settle into this lesson and bring it to reality, including the enhancement of the following "fruits."

Courage

While courage is a commonly understood word, it is helpful to review the dictionary definition stated as "mental or moral strength to venture, persevere and withstand danger, fear or difficulty." Looking to the root of the word courage, we find that it is derived from the Latin *cor,* meaning "heart." Courage, then, is the union of the moral heart with the inspired mind, focused toward action and the soothing of fear. Bringing the heart and mind together, particularly by using the breath, creates a powerful internal force that can function in the present moment to do "the greatest good." Courage allows you to face the shadows of the past that have retained the memories of fear—fear of humiliation, fear of loss, fear of rejection, fear of failure, fear of death. Courage enables you to see far beyond those murky shadows to recognize the right action to take and to make the first step.

Lorraine had the courage to refuse medications for her pain because she understood that her spiritual practice required a clear mind. She did not succumb to fear or doubt even though she was entering into unknown territory. It is a circular truth that the practice of acknowledging impermanence allows the development of courage, and greater courage enables deeper work in overcoming fear. Thus growth proceeds, step-by-step, one turn after another, as the wheel of life spins.

Courage is an attribute that will be needed in the future as our society faces the many challenges that lie ahead. Truly courageous acts are not rash or destructive, but require thoughtfulness and a commitment to do "the right thing." True courage, uniting the reasoning abilities of the mind with the moral conscience of the heart, will inspire us to find solutions to climate change that will respect the welfare of all of earth's inhabitants. True courage will also enable us to rebalance the world's economy without exploiting its most vulnerable societies and to find peaceful settlements to conflicts by rising above the shadow of fear and creating a unified vision of growth for all. This joining of the mind and heart is a crucial task if we are to prolong the survival of mankind on this planet.

Integrity

When the heart and mind are united within an individual or a society, the next natural step is to achieve greater wholeness or integrity. Integrity not only means adherence to a moral code but also means completeness or being whole. Bringing diverse parts together, including those that have previously been lost in the shadow, helps to develop greater integrity.

Once again, there is a noticeable lack of integrity in many of our society's systems. Organizations and corporations often function as separate and distinct entities to seek only their own short-term gain without awareness of the interconnectedness of life or the needs of the whole society. This lack of both moral behavior and integrated action has led to the stock market collapse, the housing crisis, and the failure of many banks. Integrity is present when wholeness exists, when nothing is left out, ignored or taken away. The act of integration also entails being incorporated and unified into a larger whole where the needs of the whole are recognized and honored. When completeness and integrity become the goals of a system, leaving nothing out, proper inspiration and right actions are the result.

The opposite of integration is compartmentalization that separates systems into isolated parts, preventing them from communicating and informing one another. Many examples of compartmentalization can be found in our society, such as a minister who denounces homosexuality even while secretly practicing this lifestyle or a politician who touts the sanctity of marriage while committing clandestine adultery. When you keep your wounds and resentments hidden within the shadow rather than bringing them to light, you foster a compartmentalization that prevents you from acting with integrity. Until you learn to manage your fear, you will experience this separation of parts, because your only answer to fear is to wall it off and lock it away. All unethical and immoral behavior springs from incompleteness and can only be corrected by overcoming fear and reintegrating that energy into the whole. Using your courage, you must expose your own Shadow, face the pain that has been twisted and knotted there for years, and bring those parts of yourself back into your conscious awareness. With awareness comes healing and reintegration. As individuals we cannot seek to act with integrity if we do not explore our shadow; and we cannot hope to heal our society's lack of integration if we do not heal ourselves first.

Consistency

When behavior is increasingly driven by integrity, the next attribute that will develop is consistency, which means "agreement or harmony of parts without contradiction." Consistency ensures that our behavior matches our internal wholeness in every situation, across time. In order to impact society and the world in a meaningful way, we must demonstrate this steady agreement in everything we do, within our organizations and ourselves. Vacillation and uncertainty will undermine our efforts and destroy our credibility, so consistency is a trait worth cultivating.

The seeming contradiction between the concepts of impermanence and consistency is important to explain. We must experience consistency in our attitude and behavior, even while we acknowledge that nothing lasts. Therefore our actions should be always motivated by the highest good, while at the same time we must exhibit no attachment or clinging to the results of our actions. To live with this paradox we must again find a balance between putting all our honest effort into a cause and letting go of a desire for a specific outcome for that effort. So if we would hope to find a solution to global climate change, we must put forth our best and purest work from our highest potential. and then we must surrender that work to the mystery of the unknown. All the while we must acknowledge and accept that our efforts might fail and that nothing is permanent. If we aspire to heal an illness, we must engage ourselves fully in the work of healing while having no expectations for the end result of that work. While it seems impossible to our linear minds to live with both of these demands, it is the hallmark of spiritual growth to present such a paradox for us to master.

In the story that began this chapter, Lorraine demonstrated great consistency in her behavior and attitude throughout her adult life. Her approach to the diagnosis of cancer was just the same as her approach to writing a poem, traveling to Europe, doing laundry, or drinking a cup of tea. In every action she undertook she devoted herself, heart, mind, body, and spirit, to giving her very best effort from the highest wisdom that was available to her in each moment. What was important to her was the quality of her action and the integrity of her being within present time. Simultaneously, she completely let go of any desires and expectations for the outcome of her effort. She chose instead to relax and allow the mystery to unfold, acknowledging all the while that nothing lasts. To live in such a manner seems nearly impossible, but we have Lorraine's story to provide a beacon of hope for learning this balance. In the end, Lorraine's suffering from her metastatic cancer was not only manageable, but became an inspiration for further growth for her. Lorraine was able to tolerate her own suffering while she also gave solace and understanding to everyone else around her. Lorraine's life and death perfectly demonstrated that if we want to heal our world we must do our own work first.

Fulfillment

The final "fruit" of accepting impermanence is the state of fulfillment that Jesus attained as He gave up His breath upon the cross. To fulfill is to make full, to bring to an end, and to develop the full potential. It is within our human nature to seek fulfillment in our lives and much of our searching and longing is toward this goal. However, we have a poor understanding of the meaning of fulfillment and spend much of our time chasing after it in the wrong places.

We have already seen that fear creates compartmentalization and prevents integration of all the diverse parts of the self. In this way, fear is an obstacle to fulfillment because it disallows completeness within. For many individuals the search for fulfillment is linked to fear—fear of emptiness, fear of meaninglessness, and fear of death. In these cases, fulfillment is mistakenly thought to be the antidote for fear. However fulfillment can never be attained when fear is the driving force behind the action. A frustrating cycle of misery results when fear leads to incomplete action which causes even more fear and more misguided action. Fulfillment cannot occur until fear is managed with courage that leads to integrated and consistent behavior. Using Jesus as an example, it is clear that His life and death exemplified all of these traits of courage, integrity, and consistency. Fulfillment of His life actually occurred with His agonizing death on the cross, which is not an outcome we would consider desirable for our own lives. But the lesson of impermanence demands acceptance of the fact that nothing lasts, and as shown in the previous lesson, we must surrender to that condition.

Our own individual definitions of fulfillment usually include achieving success, happiness, wealth, and gratification. Often we seek to fill our emptiness with material possessions, exhilarating experiences or intoxicating acclaim. However, since nothing is permanent, all of those entities fade away and leave us empty again, still searching for something to fill us.

Even when you try to find fulfillment through spiritual practice, if you are motivated in any way by fear, you will not achieve what you are seeking. Fulfillment can only exist when the certainty of death is acknowledged in every moment. Bringing death and the fear it engenders up from the shadows is necessary in order to fill the void you experience within. Death must be kept always within your vision as a wise teacher, not a terrifying stranger to lock away. If your motivation for living is to avoid death at all costs, you will be sadly disappointed in the end. But if, like Jesus and Lorraine, your manifestation of life embraces death as well, you can experience fulfillment in every moment. You are called to keep in mind the awareness that you might die at any time. But then you must toss away any worry that accompanies that awareness as you go about your routine tasks.

For example, in this moment my awareness contains the fact that I am going to die and it could happen at any time. But my awareness also contains the fact that it doesn't matter, because right now I am writing a book and I must give that action my best and highest effort. Holding both of those thoughts constantly in my awareness, I am experiencing fulfillment in this and every moment. And so, fulfillment, like Purpose, exists in the present moment, not in the future. Fulfillment cannot be attained by seeking and grasping, but by surrendering and breathing right now, in the present.

As we reach the conclusion of the *What Really Matters*, another type of fulfillment has occurred. The teachings provided to us by those whose lives have already ended have taken us from the threshold of our *Suffering*, through the broken heart of *Love* and *Forgiveness*, to dwell in *Paradise* and find our *Purpose* by *Surrendering* to *Impermanence*. These wise teachers have found fulfillment of their own suffering and dying by sharing their stories and hopefully inspiring us to live from our highest selves, manifesting all that is great and good within our humanness.

THE VIEW FROM THE GARDEN

Accept that impermanence is necessary in order for growth to occur. Scrutinize your spiritual practice for hidden motives and agendas. Use your breath to practice the "little deaths" and purify your body, mind, and spirit. Inspiration breathes new life and ideas into the mind, so use it to balance your fear. Utilize death as a teacher and savor each moment of life as if it is your last. Courage results from uniting your heart and mind and can expose and reintegrate your Shadow. Strive for consistency between your external behavior and your internal wholeness. Fulfillment cannot occur until your fear is managed with courage.

THE VIEW FROM THE GALAXY

"I am hanging in the balance
of the reality of man
Like every sparrow falling,
like every grain of sand."

-Bob Dylan

From the lofty perspective of the outer reaches of the Universe, we survey the lesson of impermanence to gain the highest wisdom available to us. While our existence on this planet, in the garden, is defined by the tension between life and death, in the spiritual realm there is no death.

There is simply the transfer of energy from one state to another. On Earth, everything physical dies, but that which is energy, the Spirit, lives on, incorporated into a new manifestation. This is hardly comforting news to us because we are so strongly identified with our physical form. But as we become more comfortable with the idea of impermanence, we may be able to perceive the Divine wisdom in this plan. The body is a vehicle for the Spirit, temporarily engaged during this brief passage on Earth for the purpose of learning valuable lessons. When we surrender to the mystery of Life we are uniting ourselves with a higher purpose. We are opening willingly to maximize our learning on Earth while we recognize that everything is impermanent except the Spirit that has been embodied. In the spiritual realm impermanence is a gift to be appreciated, for it enables passing on from this garden existence to a higher state.

In a beautiful demonstration of the concept of impermanence, Tibetan Buddhist monks engage in the making of sand mandalas, a ritual that is believed to enable healing and purification. A mandala is a circular geometric design that contains tightly balanced elements that are rich with symbolism and meaning. During this practice, a group of monks take several days to construct a mandala from sand of many different colors by painstakingly pouring the grains into an intricate pattern. When the task is completed the mandala is consecrated, and then the sand is swept up and deposited into a body of flowing water. In an instant, the tedious and time-consuming work of many hands is destroyed by those very same hands; nothing remains of the beautiful creation. But the monks carry out the work of sweeping up the sand with the same diligence and equanimity they applied while constructing the work of art.

In a similar manner, in life on this planet nature carries out acts of both creation and destruction with equal intensity, care, and non-attachment. We are asked to live our lives in harmony with this level of commitment to impermanence. We should maximize our effort in every moment, give everything we have to manifesting beauty in our earthly garden, and then allow it to be swept away in a single instant with no regret or fear. Such a task requires a lifetime of study and practice.

Our physical existence is like the sand that gets swept away as the mandala is destroyed. It is unique and beautiful in its own composition, though it is fleeting and passes away quickly. When you stand on the beach near water's edge you can feel the shifting sand beneath your feet, washing into shore with one wave and then out again with another wave.

When you try to grasp the sand in your hand it slips through your fingers as quickly as you squeeze them together. When viewed from the galaxy, it becomes apparent that we are the grains of sand sliding, one by one, through the narrow isthmus of the hourglass of the Universe. That brief and slender passage represents our lifetime on this planet, a mere transfer station from one state to another. It is not possible to stop the transition from one form to the next, and within the galaxy perspective it is totally absurd to seek to interfere with this perfect flow of life, for the cycle of Life and Death allows constant, eternal creation and manifestation. That we wish to suspend this Divine creative motion is evidence of our limited awareness, our earth-bound vision, and our painful lack of wholeness.

My work with hospice patients was a continual reminder of impermanence, requiring me to let go over and over again as each and every patient left this garden behind. Though I ached with the loss of each patient I was equally blessed by the sweetness of their last days. As told in these stories, some patients turned my life around with the lessons they brought to me. And some of them provided me with a final gift, even in their death.

*   *   *

Andy, the man whose face had been eaten by cancer, came to me in a dream near the time of his death. In this dream he appeared whole and healthy, his face intact and glowing with light. His ravaged physical body lay silently on a hospital bed nearby. I looked on as Andy covered the body with a sheet and then turned to me to say, "I came here to thank you." Pointing to his abandoned body, he added "You cared for me like God." I awoke in the morning knowing that Andy had made it through the narrow passage and entered the other side where he was complete and totally fulfilled.

*   *   *

In another dream I ascended on an elevator to a rotating restaurant atop the roof of a very high building. There I encountered Danny, the young man who died of AIDS in an earlier story. He was wearing a top hat and black tails, his body fully restored and skin free of lesions. His face glowed with transparent light as he asked me to dance with him. We laughed and twirled to the music of a twelve-piece orchestra, as Danny and I spun around and around the perimeter of the room, looking up through the glass ceiling to see millions of stars swirling overhead. While we continued to spin faster and faster, completely overtaken by the joy of the moment, the restaurant disappeared and we were twirling among the stars in rhythm with the music of the Universe.

*   *   *

As you seek to face your fears and find comfort with impermanence, remember that life is a circle, turning forever without beginning or end. Your fears of loss and failure and death are all illusions, created by focusing too closely on the garden without recognizing the view from the galaxy.

WHAT REALLY MATTERS ABOUT IMPERMANENCE

Impermanence completes your circular path to the Divine.
Face your fear of death, recognizing that death makes
creation possible.

Part III

◈

The Harvest

LIVING THE LESSONS

"The harvest is great
and the laborers are few..."

-Luke 10:2

Now that you have finished reading the 7 Lessons and have been touched and inspired by the beautiful stories of the dying, it is time to focus on the work of the garden. For all lessons, no matter how powerful or poignant, are only mental concepts until you breathe life into them and put them into action. Living the lessons consists of working through the necessary tasks of each step in order to learn, grow, and eventually harvest the benefits. But as Jesus pointed out in this statement He made to his disciples, there are few who undertake this labor even though the rewards are abundant.

Recall that in the Aramaic language every word has multiple meanings from many different aspects and so the word "harvest" can refer to the results of our efforts from physical, mental, emotional and spiritual levels. In order for each of us to harvest our highest potential our efforts must be directed both *internally* and *externally*. When we focus on improving our inner life, by smoothing out the knots and tangles of resentment we carry with us from the past, our outward behavior also becomes smoother, calmer and more compassionate. And as we give our energy to the cultivation of our relationships with others and the creation of positive outcomes in the world, we can experience greater peace and satisfaction within. In addition, our *external* struggles and challenges in relating to others help point out to us where we need more *internal* work by exposing our hidden knots and tangles.

Maintaining a balance between inner and outer work is of utmost importance, for the emphasis of one aspect of our growth over another will lead us astray. Excessive focus on outward behavior without the necessary inner work can lead to actions that appear positive on the surface but lack a stable foundation and soon fall apart. To overemphasize our own internal growth while ignoring external relationships can result in arrogant and self-righteous behavior as we fail to take responsibility for our conduct in the world.

The following story describes this process of growing both internally and externally and the struggle to remain in balance. As the final story of this book it intertwines all 7 of the lessons and demonstrates the challenge of bringing each lesson to life.

THE HOLLYHOCK MIRACLES

My years in hospice work offered me many opportunities to learn the truths taught by our living and dying and gradually inspired me to grow spiritually. During that time I worked closely with two specific patients whose lives intertwined with mine over a two-year span of time, challenging me to work through each of the 7 Lessons and apply them to my own day-to-day life. In the end, it was the simple hollyhock flower that brought us together and led each of us to transform in our own unique manner with perfect timing and rhythm.

Suffering

Before I visited Janice for the first time I had been warned that she hated doctors. She was a fifty-year-old woman who had been dealing with breast cancer for seven years and had become angry and bitter toward the medical profession. She had reluctantly agreed for me to see her and I knew that winning her trust would be a challenge. But it was important that I establish a bond with her in order to help manage her care for the last few months of her life. Because her cancer had already metastasized to her bones, she was likely to encounter a great deal of pain that would be worsened by her unresolved anger. Helping Janice face her suffering was one of the tasks that confronted our hospice team and it could not be accomplished without creating some sort of relationship with her.

Janice lived alone in a tiny, dilapidated apartment in a rundown part of town where she survived on a small amount of money allotted to her each month by her estranged husband. Though she had very little means, she kept her place immaculately clean and had carefully decorated the rooms with special keepsakes. As I began my first visit with her, Janice was tense and uncomfortable. She watched me with distrustful eyes and answered my questions tersely.

She clearly did not want me to be there and was reluctant to cooperate. I was trying so hard to say the right things that I became more and more nervous as the time passed, which caused her to become even more suspicious of me. As an awkward silence filled the room, I said a desperate little prayer in my head, "God, help me out here!"

Then, seemingly from nowhere, Janice spoke wistfully as she gazed up at the ceiling, "When I was a little girl I used to love making dolls out of hollyhock blossoms I picked from my mother's garden." And then, after a pause, "I wonder why that memory came to me just now?"

Her comment startled me as my own mind was instantly flooded with memories of making hollyhock dolls. I too had cherished that activity as a child. My mother and I would sit on the cool grass in the shade of our crabapple tree and fasten a hollyhock bud onto an inverted blossom with a toothpick. Then, after adding another blossom for a hat, we would twirl the lovely ladies around and around as if they were dancing at an elegant ball. I was so moved by the memory that my cheeks flushed red as I told Janice that she and I had shared the very same experience in our childhoods. Transported briefly to a sweet time of life, we smiled at one another and Janice finally let down her guard. Her face and her words softened as she began talking openly about her cynicism toward life and her fear of dying alone. Through a shared memory I had gained her trust, bonding with the innocent and vulnerable child that still existed within, filled with hope and the possibility of transformation.

That simple hollyhock connection had provided the key necessary to unlock the door to Janice's soul. Hollyhocks in folklore are said to have magical powers that help us learn necessary lessons; and by attracting the resources we need and adjusting internal energies, hollyhocks are thought to create change in our lives. For Janice and me, on that day a relationship began that would lead each of us to significant learning and profound change. The hollyhock magic was just beginning.

Love

A few months after I met Janice, another challenging patient was admitted to our hospice service. Addie was 84 years old and suffering from severe heart disease. She lived with her daughter Sharon who had retired early from her job in order to be a full-time caregiver for her mother. Addie quickly gained a reputation with our staff for being hostile and difficult to work with. She complained constantly and harshly criticized Sharon and our staff members for the care they were providing. Our nurses and home health aides dreaded the days they had to visit Addie because she made their jobs miserable. During a staff meeting our nursing director, who had years of hospice experience, reminded us, "People die the way they've lived." In other words, Addie's last days would probably be unpleasant because she had lived her entire adult life in anger and bitterness.

When I called on Addie for the first time, I was aware of her history and prepared for her wrath. I knew I would need all of my tolerance and patience throughout that visit just to complete the routine medical history and examination. While Addie's behavior toward me was antagonistic, as I had expected, I was surprised by the gentle, loving nature of her daughter Sharon. Her love for Addie was obvious as she provided her mother with kind and compassionate care, even though Addie could never be satisfied. I was intrigued that Addie could remain so angry when she was surrounded by such unconditional love, and I wondered if she could eventually be transformed by this love before she died. Then, as I was finishing up my notes for the day, Addie commented on how much she liked flowers as she stared out the window. She went on to say, wistfully, "I used to make hollyhock dolls when I was a little girl."

I was stunned that a second patient was sharing with me this memory of making hollyhock dolls! Was it just a coincidence? I told Addie that I also had this same childhood history and saw a smile on her face for the first time. She told me, with great delight, that Sharon had recently planted a hollyhock garden for her in the backyard, and she was eagerly waiting for summer to arrive when she expected the flowers to bloom. I wondered if perhaps this garden would be a way to reach Addie and help her heal some of her negativity.

Still marveling at the synchronicity of finding a hollyhock doll connection with two different patients at the same time, I said goodbye and walked out to my car. But I looked back to see that Sharon was following me with a distraught look on her face. She revealed that the florist had told her the hollyhocks would not bloom for another year. Because they were a biennial variety, these plants would have to lie dormant through the next winter before they would produce flowers in the following summer season. Sharon had not had the heart to tell Addie that she would not see them bloom, since the hollyhocks had been the only positive prospect in her life for many years. Addie's heart condition was worsening rapidly and she would not live that long. In fact, her anticipation of the flowers blooming in a few months seemed to be the only thing that was keeping her going. I understood Sharon's reluctance to tell Addie the truth and agreed to keep her secret. But I shared her concern that Addie's inevitable disappointment this summer would serve only to further break her heart and reinforce her negativity before she died.

Many thoughts and emotions flooded me as I drove home. Observing Sharon's saintly love for her mother and reliving my hollyhock days had once again stirred memories of my own mother. Since my father's suicide eight years earlier, I had distanced myself from her, unable to cope with my own grief and pain. For the first time I could see that the tragedy of losing my father had caused me to lose my mother as well. I understood and valued the practice of love in my life and I had to face the truth that I had hardened my heart as I refused to risk further pain. This hollyhock connection had been a key to unlocking my soul, but there was a great deal of work left for me to do.

Forgiveness

After my visit with Addie, I longed to tell Janice that I had met another person who was linked to us through hollyhock dolls. But, because of patient confidentiality, I could tell her nothing. I began to see Janice fairly regularly because she seemed to have more trust for me than anyone else on our staff. She confided many stories of her earlier life that helped me understand why she was so distrustful and angry. A series of traumatic events had wounded her soul and impacted the rest of her life, causing her to tightly wall off her heart for protection. I understood how, when her cancer was diagnosed, she perceived it as one more insult from God, one more sign that she didn't deserve to be loved. It seemed to me that Janice was tangled and knotted inside with resentment and anger and I couldn't imagine how to help her unravel the chaotic jumble of emotion she carried. But I recognized that all of her vital energy was being consumed by this black hole of misery inside of her. In addition, her emotional pain altered her view of everything in her world; no matter what happened to her she could see only the negative aspect of the experience. Even a kind gesture or gift from another person would be distorted in her mind into an insult or attack.

Drawing from my experiences with other hospice patients, I attempted to talk with Janice about the idea of forgiveness, suggesting that she might need to work on this process so she could die peacefully. But practicing forgiveness made no sense to her at all. From her perspective the act of forgiving others would "let them off the hook" and that seemed totally unfair. She had invested her energy in seeking revenge against those who had harmed her, and it would take a lot of work to help Janice see the benefit in releasing her anger to reconcile her relationships and let go of her old wounds.

Though I could speak with others passionately about the need to forgive, I discovered during those days that I was not very good at achieving it myself. I would listen to my own words and know that they were true, but I had no idea how to begin healing my own tangled resentment. However, recognition of the problem is the first step toward resolution, so at least I had begun to work on the task I needed to accomplish. In my talks with Janice I was reminded many times of the hollyhock dolls and how that connection had bonded us from the beginning. I was starting to recognize that it was not just a random coincidence but an opportunity for deep healing that had arisen both for Janice and for me.

Paradise

As the days of spring gave way to the heat of summer over the next few months, Addie's physical condition continued to decline. But she was still fighting to hold on until July, when she expected her hollyhocks to bloom. No one had yet been courageous enough to tell her those plants required the freezing darkness of winter in order to bring forth their glorious flowers. But Addie seemed to have entered a darkness of her own, as she began experiencing terrifying nightmares each time she tried to sleep. Her description of these dreams reminded me of scenes from Dante's Inferno with her visions of horror, destruction, violence, and suffering. Nothing we tried could alleviate these night terrors for Addie and it seemed that they were perhaps part of her process of reconciling her life. She actually tolerated fairly well these "dark dreams," as she called them, and according to the nurses her temperament in the daytime seemed to be softening a little.

After a month or so, in early July, Addie's nightmares stopped abruptly, just as they had started and for no apparent reason. Within a few more days, she began sleeping most of the day as she entered into the "active dying" phase that is so characteristic of hospice patients at the end of life. I visited Addie one last time and found her peacefully sleeping, though she opened her eyes and greeted me with a luminous smile when she heard my voice. I had never seen her face look so beautiful and radiant and I could not take my eyes off her. She told me a man had come and taken her dark dreams away and that he was now sitting on the chair in her room, waiting for her. Glancing at the empty chair in the corner, I recognized that Addie was having an end-of-life vision, as I had witnessed with many other patients in the past. She added, "Look, doctor, my hollyhock," pointing to a single pink hollyhock blossom floating in a crystal bowl on the nightstand. I assumed that Sharon, in her loving and thoughtful manner, had retrieved a hollyhock blossom from a neighbor's yard so that her mother's wish could be fulfilled. Yet when I glanced at Sharon I saw that tears were streaming down her face and she was nodding affirmatively. "They bloomed! The hollyhocks really bloomed!" she assured me.

Saying my farewell to Addie, who had returned to her state of sleep, I followed Sharon to the backyard. There, to my astonishment, against the fence was a stunning array of yellow, red, purple, pink, and white hollyhocks in their fullest bloom. Each tall fuzzy stem was covered with dozens of blossoms, and as a gentle breeze blew they swayed in the wind like beautifully gowned ladies at an elegant ball.

From my research I know that it is possible under extreme circumstances for biennial plants to bloom out of season. But on that day the sight of those hollyhocks, so abundant and lavish in that garden, was to me a true miracle. For all her bitterness and negativity, Addie had clung to only one hope for the future, to just the one positive vision that she would see those hollyhocks bloom. And much to our surprise, she was not disappointed. Her heart was not shattered, but was lovingly held as she received exactly what she needed to die a peaceful death. Addie's garden on the day of her death was Paradise, a Heaven brought to Earth, for the benefit of all. Everything had been perfect, after all, just as it was meant to be.

Purpose

The blooming of Addie's hollyhocks had given me new hope and inspiration for working with Janice. I believed more than ever that our three paths had crossed for a reason and that Heaven would provide Janice with whatever she needed to transform before her death. But I didn't realize that it might take a very long time, with diligent work and infinite patience for that transformation to occur. In fact, at the time of Addie's death, Janice had already been with hospice for a year. Her cancer was still progressing, but very slowly, as if her life were being held in suspended animation to allow her a chance to do the spiritual work she needed to accomplish.

Just as the hollyhocks need the cold and darkness of winter in order to bloom, Janice had to face some additional difficulties, as well. During that same summer her insurance benefit for hospice care expired and she had to be discharged from our services. I was particularly worried about this turn of events, knowing that it would only feed her negative view of life and God. In addition, the pharmacy that provided her medications was located thirty miles from her home and did not have a delivery service. Janice had been dependent on our staff to bring her prescriptions to her every two weeks and had no one else in her life who could perform this service for her. Our social worker called every volunteer agency in the community but found no help available. This situation became a crisis point for me as I struggled to find a solution. I didn't want to give up on Janice and, in fact, felt that I had an obligation to keep working with her. In the end I decided to take over the task of delivering her prescriptions. I would go to the pharmacy every two weeks and bring her medications to her apartment as a voluntary act of service. While this was outside the bounds of my usual work as a doctor, I felt that it was the right thing for me to do. It was my highest purpose for that particular situation.

So every other Wednesday morning, after taking my children to school, I would drive to the pharmacy, drop off the prescriptions and wait for them to be filled. Because it was an extremely busy military pharmacy, the wait time for prescription pick-up was one to two hours, so I spent that time sitting in the reception area. However, rather than being a source of stress for me, the waiting actually became part of my spiritual process. I would sit quietly and observe other people there, sometimes writing in my journal, reading, or meditating. The main focus of that time was to just be still, to exist in the present moment. By quieting my thoughts and forcing myself to sit in one place, which was a rare occurrence in my busy life, I created an opportunity for many emotions and insights to rise to the surface. On those Wednesday mornings I began to look at my own resentments, to recognize the wounds from which they arose and experience the compassion that would eventually help me untangle and smooth those knots I was carrying within. Much of the work I did focused on my anger toward my mother and my continued grief over my father's death. When the prescriptions were ready I would drive to Janice's apartment, arriving there in a state of serenity, ready to listen and reflect with her.

The change that was taking place inside of me seemed to have a positive impact on my conversations with Janice. I became more spontaneous and better able to see through her pain to the shining of her Divine soul. At times I could connect with the deepest part of her and see glimpses of realization light up her face. Meanwhile, my own soul was benefiting from the steady, regular work I was carrying out with my highest level of integrity and diligence. I held myself accountable for making sure Janice had her medications on time, and the firmness of that expectation created boundaries and structure for my growth process, requiring me to do the necessary work even when I lacked motivation. On Wednesday mornings, the pharmacy waiting area became a sort of monastery for me while sitting quietly became my spiritual practice.

In this way Janice and I continued to work together, helping one another heal and untangle the twisted places inside by simply meeting on a regular basis. I understood that it was not my intellect or medical knowledge that made a difference to Janice. It was merely my ability to be present in the moment that impacted her. Together we were journeying into unknown territory, and in spite of our frailty and weaknesses and illnesses, we were providing one another with the courage and strength necessary to continue. Throughout this time I recognized that the hollyhock connection that bound us together in the first place had been an essential factor for the healing and growth of each of us. And the link with Addie and her garden had been necessary as well to bolster my faith and reinforce my commitment to Janice. Whether due to hollyhock magic or random coincidence or divine intervention, change was happening for both Janice and me as we worked together with loving care and authenticity, manifesting our highest potential for those brief moments suspended in present time.

Surrender

Months passed by as I waited quietly in the pharmacy every other Wednesday and then met with Janice for the following hour. She was making progress toward repairing some of her damaged relationships and I was recognizing my own displaced guilt and shame over my father's death. While her health was gradually declining, it still seemed as if Janice's cancer had been temporarily suspended so that she could do this important work. Almost unnoticed, another year had passed by when a sudden change appeared on the horizon. My husband received an offer for employment in a different community and as a family we had decided to move to a neighboring state. We put our house on the market immediately, making plans to leave within a few weeks so that our children could start school in our new town. I was both excited for this new opportunity and devastated to abandon Janice. She had made so much progress over the past year and I feared it would all be destroyed when I left, confirming her old belief that she is worthless and no one really cares about her.

I couldn't understand why life had unfolded in this manner. I had believed that everything would work out for Janice and that she would have whatever she needed, but now that idea seemed false. Instead, she would be broken again, and I would be the cause. But finally I had no choice except to surrender to the circumstances, for I couldn't change the past or the future. I could only let go and flow with the present moment, accepting whatever came to pass.

When I delivered the news to Janice she listened carefully with no reaction whatsoever. Then she turned to face the wall and I waited for a seeming eternity before she spoke, "I've always thought you would be here with me until I died." Yes, I had always thought the same thing. Why was it not working out? What had gone wrong? I left her apartment that day with a promise to visit one more time before our move, but I had no assurance that this situation could have a positive resolution. Later that same day, however, I received a phone call from Janice's daughter, Tina. Janice had been reaching out to her as part of her healing work over the past few months. Tina had just been furloughed from her job and wanted to become more involved in her mother's care. I was relieved to learn that at the very least, Tina would be there after I left to look in on Janice and pick up her prescriptions.

When I made my final visit to Janice I found that she was, as I had feared, in a state of anger. But she directed all of it toward God, whom she felt had let her down repeatedly in her life. She believed that God had never cared about her and never touched her life. This was the deepest core of her rage, at the foundation of all her other wounds. I tried to point out the good things that had happened for her over the past year, including Tina becoming involved in her life again. Finally, I decided to tell her the rest of the hollyhock story, hoping that she would see that as a sign of God's presence in her life. I told her about Addie's garden and the miraculous blooming of her hollyhocks just before her death. Janice was amazed and speechless for a few moments and then whispered, "God made those hollyhocks bloom for her so she would know He loved her. It was a sign." I was thrilled that she had grasped that point. However, to my distress she turned her face to the wall again stating, "God has never given ME a sign." Once more, her negative attitude caused her to view everything through a lens of disappointment. There was no way to comfort her. There was nothing more I could do and so that is how we left things. She refused to say goodbye and I had to walk away from her while feeling the pain of failure and loss and confusion all at once. Maybe I had been naïve to believe in the hollyhock connection. I had envisioned a happy ending for this story, but it hadn't happened that way. I would have to move on to my new life with no answers and the sting of unmet expectations as I learned the painful lesson of surrender.

Impermanence

However, a month after the move, I had an opportunity to return to our old community for an impromptu visit and decided to look in on Janice while I was there. Tina had called to let me know that Janice had taken a turn for the worse and was no longer able to get out of bed. This decline led to Tina moving into the tiny apartment with her in order to provide care around-the-clock. In the time since I had left, Janice had continued to work on forgiveness, reconciling with her son and a sister, which had been a very positive experience. Yet Tina was concerned that something was still bothering her mother that needed to be resolved and she believed that Janice needed to talk to me.

When I arrived at Janice's apartment, she was sleeping in her hospital bed that had been placed in the living room under a window overlooking a tiny deck. Janice awoke when she heard my voice and greeted me with great joy. Her face was radiant and peaceful, a look that she had never before displayed. I recognized that she had been through a profound transformation since I had left having reconciled with Tina who was now providing her with loving, devoted care. In that moment I finally understood that my leaving had been necessary in order to make space for Tina to become Janice's caregiver. The timing had been perfect after all. Janice then took my hand and thanked me for being part of her life. She also thanked me for telling her the story of Addie's hollyhocks, for she had found it to be a source of comfort over the past month. She had let go of her anger at God and now had faith that she would be given a sign whenever the time was right. Exhausted from the effort of giving me this message, Janice laid her head on the pillow and returned to a deep sleep. I sat quietly by her side until she awoke once more to say our final goodbye.

Tina called a few weeks later to report that Janice had died peacefully in her sleep the night before. However, something strange had occurred during the three days before her death. Tina had left the window next to Janice's bed open, forgetting that it had no screen. A tiny hummingbird had flown in through the window and hovered directly over Janice as it looked down at her. Tina had rushed over to shoo the bird back out the window, but Janice had stopped her, ecstatic with joy. "It's my sign," she gasped. "It's God!" Tina hadn't understood what her mother meant by that, but she honored her wish to leave the window open. During those three days, the hummingbird flitted in and out through the window multiple times. But every time Janice awoke and opened her eyes the hummingbird was there and hovered just above her, bringing her great peace and joy. At last, Janice had received the sign she longed for and knew she was loved by God and was at home in the Universe.

Shortly after I received the news of Janice's death, I dreamed of my father. He had been visiting us in our new home, quietly watching our daily activities from a distance. In the next part of the dream I went into the master bedroom to find him lying on the bed with both his arms outstretched, looking in that moment just like Jesus upon the cross. Then the figure transformed into my father's body again, but I saw, to my disappointment, that it was lifeless. I wept as I touched his cold, stiff arm, "Oh Daddy, I forgot that you died." As my grief spilled over and my tears fell upon the bedspread, Dad sat upright and took me into his arms, saying, "I came to tell you how much I love you." I awoke from that dream with the intense, burning electricity of love flowing through me. It felt as if Dad had really been in the room and his spirit was still lingering there for a moment. I too had received a sign that I am loved, that my existence matters.

A few months later I received a package in the mail from Tina. She wanted me to know that she was doing well and she was sending a few of her mother's things for me to remember her by. There was a tiny stuffed-toy dog that Janice had loved, her yellow flashlight that she always kept by her bed, and an old, unopened box of stationery

Tina had found in the back of Janice's desk. After removing the plastic covering, I took the lid off the box of stationery to find sheets of note paper decorated with a purple and pink watercolor design: a tiny hummingbird hovering in a garden of hollyhocks. It was perfect. It was all perfect and always had been. Now I could finally see it.

Setting aside the stationery I reached for the phone and dialed. "Hi Mom. I've been wanting to call you for a while. . . . Remember when we used to make hollyhock dolls in the backyard . . ."

*　　*　　*

Thus began the next phase of this journey as my mother and I reconnected with renewed compassion, understanding, and forgiveness, seeking to help one another heal the grief that had torn us apart for many years. When we could finally share our mutual pain, my anger dissolved away, replaced at last by calm acceptance and peace. Now as my mother's own health grows frail and she looks toward the end of her days, we talk sometimes about her garden and the joy it used to bring her. I have decided that this spring I will make the long trip home and help her plant some flowers once again, reviving the soil that has become hardened over many winters to unlock the potential for new life that lies waiting there.

The road to spiritual growth travels through the dangerous territory of untold suffering, unanswered questions, and unmet dreams. But we must gather our courage and take one step after another, believing it will be perfect, holding on to the ones we love, and planting a hollyhock here and there along the way.

WHAT MATTERS MOST

We shall not cease from exploration.
And the end of all our exploring
Will be to arrive where we started
And know the place for the first time.

-T. S. Eliot

While each of the 7 Lessons has demonstrated a component of What Really Matters, there is one truth that rises above all: the motivation for life is ultimately to grow spiritually, little by little, step-by-step, layer-by-layer. The impetus for growth is woven into every cell and fiber of your being. In fact, you cannot stop growth, though you can slow down the process considerably by manufacturing obstacles and languishing in your difficulties. The direction of the unfolding of life is toward maximum diversity and complexity, which you see reflected all around you in nature. But for your own personal growth as a spiritual being, the tasks you are to undertake in your garden all point toward greater simplicity. While the human mind is currently manifesting technologies of staggering intricacy and variety, Spirit is calling for the creation of balance through actions that are basic and simple, like breathing.

No matter where you find yourself in life at this time, growth is occurring within you and you can provide support or deterrence for that growth through your actions. Even if you are caught up in a cycle of self-destruction, there are inside of you the tiny seeds of change, awaiting the proper time for opening. If you choose to foster your own growth, begin wherever you are right now and take any step that is possible for you. Even the smallest bit of movement can change everything in an instant.

The 7 Lessons can provide you with a map for change, presenting you with tasks to perform and challenges to master, and they can be approached in any order that seems to fit your needs. It is important, however, to remember that learning and growth continue throughout life, so you are never finished with any single lesson. Each time you reach a new level of understanding, you must cycle back again through every step, applying your new knowledge as you go. For example, once you learn to accept impermanence and face life with less fear, you must return to your suffering, your broken heart, and your resentments in order to view those aspects of yourself through a new lens of courage. Likewise, you must reevaluate your ability to be in the present moment and manifest your potential to now experience those states with less fear attached to them. The path of spiritual growth occurs as a spiral, circling back through the same space over and over again, but moving ever upward. If you believe that you have already mastered any of the lessons, like forgiveness, for example, there is a good chance that you have buried some of those knots and tangles deep in the Shadow within where they lie in wait for an opportunity to burst forth. Keep an open mind when you look at yourself, stay humble and be prepared for some surprises.

THE LAYOUT OF THE GARDEN

In order to create a plan for your spiritual garden, it is helpful to review the 7 Lessons and their interrelationships. While a garden is composed of individual plants that require one-on-one care, the beauty and function of the entire garden depends on the arrangement and connection of all of those plants, one to another. Similarly, the steps of your spiritual growth each deserve their own individual attention, but the beauty and power of the message lies in the intertwining of all the lessons. Each lesson can be found within every other lesson, and each offers its own unique perspective on the course of spiritual growth.

To begin, suffering can be the impetus for this process as it awakens the mind to the internal longing for wholeness. In this way, illness, loss, disappointment, and tragedy can all be considered blessings when they open the door of inquiry into the mystery of life. This dynamic has been demonstrated over and over again in the stories of the dying patients you've read. Once your mind is unlocked your heart can find a little more space to begin its push toward the light of awareness. The energy of the heart is always compelled toward love and when you allow love to manifest, you will surely experience the exquisite agony of breaking open the heart's protective shell. Many times you can get waylaid by this pain and spiral downward rather than up, as you tie your heart into knots to prevent any further trauma. To find your way back to the path, you will need to loosen the knots and smooth the tangles by practicing forgiveness, over and over again, to a deeper and deeper level. When you can proceed without adding new tangles or knots to the fabric of your spiritual development, a surge of energy will become available to you, which you must use wisely and avoid squandering. If you awaken further into the recognition that only the present moment exists, which is paradise, then that energy will be available for enlivening your highest potential and creating a sense of purpose. But you must be careful to manifest that purpose with all your positive intention, and at the same time to surrender, to free yourself of all expectations, a very difficult balance to maintain. You will be aided in that quest for balance when the realization comes to you that everything is impermanent. Finally, when you can hold that reality within your awareness, you will have discovered the secret antidote to the fear that shackles you, along with a narrow, twisting trail that can lead you out of your suffering.

And so, having come full circle, you begin again with this path of growth, returning to the same markers along the way to view them each time with clearer eyes.

While this is the layout of one journey through the garden, there are an infinite number of paths possible, unique to each life. It is one of the fascinations of existence to watch each moment unfold and see the turning of the spiral before you.

The Dance of Life

As you studied each of the 7 Lessons, you may have been aware of some underlying concepts that were common to every lesson and recurred throughout the previous chapters. These are the components of the dance of life that were presented in the introduction and that anchor each lesson: timing, balance, rhythm, and grace. Keeping them in mind will be helpful as you step lightly on this tricky journey.

Timing

It has been mentioned repeatedly that spiritual growth takes time and cannot be rushed or forced. Great patience is necessary in this slowly unfolding process as change occurs little by little. In the fast pace of contemporary life you may feel as though you rarely have enough time for any of the things you value and may not be able to imagine adding more to your schedule. One of the most common excuses I hear from people who are not successful at creating change in their lives is that there simply is not enough time. This is an area where you must keep an open mind and continually redefine your concept of time. Whatever you focus your attention upon will automatically generate the time needed for its manifestation. Think about all the things you do in a single day and how there is always enough time for them to occur. If you focus upon a new activity you want to include in your day and have a sincere intention, there will be sufficient time for that activity. Other events will speed up or slide together or become simpler in order to make room for the new intention. You must stop using time as an excuse for not pursuing growth in your life. Time exists only in your mind and when you no longer view yourself as a slave to it you will be free to better manage your days.

Another important aspect of timing that has been mentioned throughout the lessons is the pace at which life unfolds. This principle was illustrated in *The Hollyhock Miracles*, as Janice worked for two years to achieve forgiveness and I struggled with grief for over a decade. The plants in the garden grow according to their own schedule, sprouting, blossoming, and going to seed at just the right time when the conditions are favorable. If you try to tamper with that timing, you risk damaging the plants or even destroying them. Your own growth is dependent upon many diverse factors, often unseen and unknown by you, coming together at just the right time in your life. When you try to rush the process or skip some of the steps, you will not really be growing at all. You will just create more tangles that will have to be straightened out later. It is far better to wait patiently for the timing to work itself out, surrendering to the unknown and letting it be.

As Lorraine, the poet with breast cancer, advised me about my writing: sometimes you are not ready to be finished; you will know it when you *are* ready. I often see people who disregard timing in their relationships, rushing into commitment without sufficient preparation, pushing to attain a level of intimacy that is not realistic at that time. Eagerness to be fulfilled can be so compelling that it overshadows the wisdom of patience. But the consequence of forcing a bond with another person or pushing a project before the timing is right is like eating unripe fruit—it can leave a bad taste in your mouth along with a seriously tangled wound that will require attention in the future.

While growth requires patience and takes a great deal of time, it is also true that transformation can occur in an instant. This is a confusing paradox of spiritual growth that makes life unpredictable and fascinating, keeping you always guessing. The trick to living within this paradoxical universe is to find a way to stay balanced in the middle.

Balance

The concept of balance has been discussed in various ways within each of the 7 lessons, for spiritual growth launches from a place of stability, even in the midst of chaos. Our existence on planet Earth is defined by pairs of opposites, including day and night, light and dark, joy and pain, good and bad. The untrained mind tends to identify with one pole or the other because it has difficulty holding onto two opposite concepts at the same time. To the linear Western mind, if one situation is *right*, then the opposite must be *wrong*, making it nearly impossible to find a middle ground. But in the higher spiritual realm, there are no such divisions. All boundaries tend to blend together and opposites are united, for both are essential in order to achieve wholeness. One goal of spiritual growth is to achieve equanimity, which is evenness of the mind, brought about by finding the stable middle ground. To move forward, you must maneuver your way to the balancing point in every possible moment.

Ultimately, balance is a concept you can apply to any situation. If you are struggling to make a decision about something, search for the middle ground; if you are losing control over your emotions, a sure sign of imbalance, take a deep breath and focus on returning to a point of stability; when caught up in conflict between groups with opposing positions, see yourself in the center with an understanding of the needs of both sides. Once you begin to recognize the point of balance, you can practice at maintaining it, which is not easily done. But as the discipline of yoga teaches, you learn balance best by continually falling out of it and returning. Hold in your thoughts a commitment to balance as you move throughout your day and keep returning to it over and over again.

Rhythm

The 7 lessons have been interspersed throughout with references to nature and its perfect rhythm, another important element of the dance of life to remember as you work on your spiritual growth. All of life pulses and vibrates with energy, continuously flowing through and around every physical form. You are made up of this energy and communicate with the Universe through your energetic fields. As you become more consciously aware, you will be able to detect the rhythm of this spiritual energy and bring your own rhythm into harmony with the rest of life. This state of harmonious rhythm is often referred to as being "in the flow" and is desired by athletes, artists, public speakers, and musicians, to name a few. Exceptional creativity and performance are possible when you are "in the flow," which is another benefit of dwelling in the present moment. Practice breathing and quieting the mind to develop your sense of this rhythm. It will also be necessary, of course, to keep clearing away the internal obstacles that interfere with staying in the present, such as resentment and fear.

Grace

The final element of the dance of life is grace, or the generosity of abundance. Several of the lessons have emphasized that giving should take priority over receiving, particularly the giving of love and forgiveness. Grace specifically means the act of giving when it is not earned or deserved, an even deeper level of generosity. While our society places enormous emphasis on acquiring and taking whatever is desired, the impulse of the Spirit, in contrast, is to give solely for the sake of giving, just as the garden provides us with abundant crops and flowers. As a human being you are naturally divided within yourself, for the heart and soul long to give, while the mind and ego are concerned with tallying what has been received. When giving is pure and free of attachment, such as the giving of love, forgiveness, presence, and intention, a harmonious connection is established with the Universe, the collective field of awareness. From this act of grace, you do have the ability to impact and alter the Universe, but you must work hard to untie the strings the mind attaches to your efforts. When you believe that your thoughts alone can control the Universe and bring you the things you desire, you are succumbing to the greed of the ego and mind. Only a focus on unselfish giving can open a space within which change can occur and miracles can blossom.

*   *   *

Timing, balance, rhythm, grace: keep these four concepts in mind and use them as a measuring stick for your actions. When you are on the right path you should recognize that you are giving without expectations, operating from a balanced mind and heart, in rhythm with the flow of energy around you, and practicing patience as you wait for the proper timing of events.

TENDING YOUR GARDEN

*"May our heart's garden of awakening
bloom with hundreds of flowers."*

-Thich Nhat Hanh

In order to foster your spiritual growth through the 7 Lessons, you must focus your time and energy on tending to your own garden. This will require you to develop some sort of *daily practice* for yourself. Your own individual routine might consist of some type of exercise, eating a specific diet, prayer, meditation, journaling, yoga, martial arts or any combination of activities. In the end, it doesn't really matter *what* you choose to practice, but it matters *how* you practice. You should always perform with *diligence*, taking special care with even the smallest and least significant tasks. Also, you must develop *consistency* in your practice to realize lasting growth and benefit. As emphasized earlier, a focus on breathing should be an aspect of your daily routine, utilizing various techniques to enhance your relaxation and the integration of body, mind, heart, and spirit.

Additionally, the basic tasks of tending your garden consist of "planting seeds, pulling weeds." Work to plant the seeds of new awareness through your daily practice, and be vigilant to search for the weeds of disowned parts of yourself that lurk in the subconscious. These weeds make up the Shadow aspect of human nature and threaten to strangle the fragile tendrils of growth in your garden. Initially, the bulk of spiritual work lies in clearing away the weeds of hidden motives, buried resentments, and unhealed grief. Do not underestimate your need to address your own Shadow. Fortunately, there are many tools that can help you identify these darker parts of yourself and bring them up to the light where they can be brought back to harmony with the soul. By engaging in positive practices for the body, mind, heart, and spirit, you can overcome the obstacles that thwart your progress toward wholeness, your true purpose on this planet. Choose those practices that best fit your belief system or lifestyle. Again, it is most important to create a daily routine that has significance for you and that you will be able to perform with dedication and passion. Following is a recommended approach to working with each lesson and the common "weeds" of the Shadow self that can undermine your progress.

Suffering

When you first begin to address your own suffering, you must face your difficulties head-on. Do not hide from your suffering or try to escape for you will only increase your misery. Attempting to numb the pain with alcohol, drugs, or other distractions will hinder your ability to grow and learn from the situations life has presented. Utilize practices such as deep breathing, meditation, and prayer to manage your fear so that it does not control your behavior. Be open to the counsel and wisdom of others, possibly joining a support group, for it is difficult to confront suffering by yourself. If necessary, use prescription medications to help you tolerate the exploration of your suffering, but not to shut out your pain. When you feel you have made progress and are ready to give to others in need, volunteer work can be helpful. Also as you move through this lesson you must commit to being honest with yourself and others and practicing humility and patience.

Self-pity is the "weed" that threatens your ability to embrace your difficulties and utilize your suffering to open the door to growth. In *The Hollyhock Miracles* both Janice and Addie were plagued by excessive self-pity that initially prevented them from coping with their life situations and moving forward. When you allow yourself to be trapped in self-pity, you cannot see beyond your own misery; your mind focuses excessively on your pain, causing it to become even more exaggerated. While it is necessary to acknowledge suffering in order to attend to it, you must take care to move on and redirect your attention to avoid getting caught in the trap of self-pity.

Love

Begin to learn the lesson of love by recognizing that every connection in your life has something to offer. Have the mindset to discover who in your world is waiting to experience the sharing of love with you. Even if you are alone, open your mind and heart to others so you can see opportunities to give and receive genuine love. You will find that they are all around you. While practicing guided imagery, meditation, or prayer, visualize your heart opening to allow love to flow freely in and out. You must eventually permit yourself to be vulnerable in your deepest relationships by focusing first on what you can give to others rather than on what you can receive. Begin with small acts of generosity as you gradually expand your capacity to give, though you must be certain that your actions are carried out with authenticity. Look for the light of the Divine in everyone and everything, but first find a way to love yourself that is not selfish and embraces the presence of the Divine within you. Watch for small miracles to occur in your everyday life and record them in your journal so you can refer back to it when times are more difficult.

Self-sufficiency, while generally thought to be a positive trait, can be an obstacle to achieving true love because it resists the brokenness that is necessary for opening the heart. When you rely excessively on your own abilities to solve every problem and you exclude others from engaging with you in a meaningful way, you prevent the vulnerability that love requires in order to blossom. In our hollyhock story Janice had survived a difficult life by becoming extremely self-sufficient. However, that survival tactic eventually worked against her. She became incapable of allowing others into her life until illness broke down her barriers and opened her heart to the love she needed. You must learn to balance self-sufficiency with openness so that you can truly give and receive love with others in your life.

Forgiveness

Begin your approach by identifying the major issues in your life that require you to forgive yourself, others, and God. Recognize that holding onto resentment is poisonous to your own soul and healing past wounds may actually help improve your physical health. You must take responsibility for your own behavior in the past and the present, acknowledging mistakes you've made; then focus on letting go of your own regret and seeing the perfection in everything. Apply this same technique to everyone in your life, letting go over and over again of the pain you have stored away inside. Journaling, prayer, and meditation are very helpful practices for moving toward forgiveness. Focus on creating a "clean slate" within as you let go of past resentments. Also consider utilizing a physical action to signify your forgiveness, which was helpful to some of the patients in earlier stories. You might benefit from creating a small shrine or forgiveness garden, writing a poem, drawing a picture, or being of service to someone else.

The pitfall that undermines the practice of forgiveness is *privilege*, which means to view oneself as different from others and therefore not subject to the same rules. Though the word is often used to describe those of an elite upper class, an excessive sense of privilege can actually afflict anyone of any social status. For example, Addie's constant outrage in the hollyhock story arose from a belief that she, unlike every other living thing, should not have to suffer. When you believe that you are entitled to special or different treatment you become unable to release from blame those who may have done harm to you. The attitude of privilege creates the false assumption that nothing bad should ever happen to you, only to other people. Forgiveness, which is based on the belief that everything that occurs in your life is perfect in its own way, becomes impossible until you recognize your connection with every other living being and humbly assume your role in the unfolding of life.

Paradise

Remaining in the present moment will be one of your most difficult spiritual tasks, but any small amount of progress made can have great impact. Use reminders, such as a small bracelet on your wrist or notes to yourself in your workspace, to help you bring your attention over and over again back to the present moment. You must spend time in meditation or prayer every day to practice focusing your attention. Utilize mundane tasks, such as washing dishes or doing laundry, as an opportunity to improve your ability to be present. Instead of day-dreaming during these activities, bring your full concentration to them, noticing the small details detected by your senses, such as touch, smell, or sound. You might benefit from spending time in nature, free of your daily distractions, and tuning in to the rhythm of life, always unfold-ing in the present moment. When you catch yourself worrying about the future or mulling over the past, stop everything and take a deep breath. Remind yourself that none of these thoughts matter right now in this moment and feel the relief of dwelling in present time, even if only briefly. Trust that you will have what you need for growth at just the right time.

Grief that has persisted without proper healing is the weed that interferes with living in the paradise of the present moment. Unresolved pain from loss and trauma lurks in the subconscious where it traps your energy in the past and poisons your ability to be productive in the pres-ent, resulting in physical and psychological illness. In my own situation, as shown in the hollyhock story, unhealed grief over my father's death kept me caught in a cycle of busyness, always worrying about the future or regretting the past and unable to participate in love or forgiveness in the present moment. When a situation arose that forced me to confront the present moment, I was finally able to begin the process of healing. Sometimes grief that is appropriate when it initially arises ends up being ignored or buried and not given the opportunity to properly resolve. This occurs in our society because of our discomfort with the magnitude of suffering that arises from loss and a lack of adequate tools for coping with grief. Instead, the pain becomes buried in the subconscious where it undermines health and growth. To truly live in the present moment, escaping the chasm of the past, it is necessary to unearth grief and seek resolution for the pain.

Purpose

In order to live your highest potential in the present moment you will have to alter your definitions of success and meaning, accepting the fact that your true purpose may be something different than you had thought. Ultimately you must also free yourself from expectations of achievement and acquisition. However, rather than trying to eliminate your desire for more things and higher status, you should work on developing compassion toward the parts of yourself that are unfulfilled. Then focus more intently on staying in the present moment and in balance, even while making necessary plans for the future. Remember that you co-create your path, one step at a time, but the outcome of that path is a mystery until it arrives. Be willing to start over an infinite number of times with the intention to just be your highest possible self. Strive to do everything with diligence and then hold yourself accountable for the results by reflecting on them in your journal. During prayer or meditation you may benefit from using the images of clarity, such as a cloudless sky or deep pool of still water as mental reminders that your purpose is simple and already within you.

The manifestation of purpose is most threatened by the "weed" of *ambition*, the desire for status, fame, or power. When your ego seizes upon a goal for the future that is inspired by greed for more attention or attainment, the true purpose of your life can be obscured and overlooked. During my work with Janice, as recounted in the story *The Hollyhock Miracles*, my true purpose was manifested through the lowly act of sitting in a pharmacy waiting room, a task that had nothing to do with my ambition to be a successful physician. In the end I had to be willing to suspend that ambition and accept the simple calling that was put before me in order to become the person I was meant to be. Setting aside ambitious goals is a difficult challenge that requires you to be diligent in analyzing your underlying motives. You must bring to light your secret and grand desires, keeping them always in your vision as you focus on the present moment. Then, within the light of your awareness, your ambition can be converted to healthy inspiration.

Surrender

In order to truly surrender you must spend time in contemplation and journaling to bring to light your fear and greed. It will be helpful to you to review the previous lessons in order to determine where you still need to clear away the clutter of old resentments and limiting ideas. Then you will need to revisit those areas and continue experiencing forgiveness until you release more of your energy from the past. Practices such as tai chi and dance can help you reduce your self-consciousness and learn to move the body in rhythm. Creative activities like painting, writing or making music allow you to experience moments of true surrender. You can also utilize "don't-know mind" to counteract the tendency to overanalyze the past and future, reminding yourself, "I don't know." Become more aware of synchronous events in your life and make note of them in your journal.

Your ability to practice surrender can be undermined by *pride*, which is defined as having an excessive attachment to self-esteem. The ego's expression of pride consists of an attitude of "I know best," preventing you from letting go of your expectations for the future. In the hollyhock story when the opportunity for my family to move to another state disrupted my work with Janice, both she and I were forced to surrender, though it went against what we each believed to be the best outcome. Accepting that disruption and allowing it to unfold challenged my pride and I struggled to trust that it could be the right thing. I was certain that "I knew best" and that life had somehow made a mistake until it was revealed to me that everything worked out perfectly. In order to learn the lesson of surrender, you must address your pride and detach your self-esteem from the expectation of knowing everything. Instead, cultivate within yourself respect for not knowing and rest patiently in the unknown.

Impermanence

Finally, in order to prepare yourself to live with the knowledge of impermanence, you must focus on bringing all the hidden parts of yourself out of the shadow and into the light of awareness. You must engage in a consistent contemplative practice such as prayer or journaling because achieving this awareness requires constant effort. Work toward becoming more integrated by practicing yoga or other types of bodywork that bring together the body, mind, heart, and spirit. Actively seek to listen to both your heart and mind when making decisions, being aware of the fact that they may often be at odds with one another. To experience impermanence in your daily life, awaken early enough to watch the sunrise and enjoy the fleeting beauty of the break of day. Also, acknowledge impermanence whenever you perform housework, which becomes undone just as soon as you finish it. Observe the levels of courage and consistency that are present in your own behavior and attitude, then work to improve them by uniting the compartmentalized parts of yourself.

Doubt is the pitfall that swallows up your intention to live the lesson of impermanence. Doubt arises from an unstable mind that has not yet been brought into harmony with the spirit, heart, and body. Janice struggled with her doubt throughout the hollyhock story and I experienced doubt, as well, when I believed that Addie's hollyhocks would not bloom and that Janice would not transform if I moved away. For each of us, doubt undermined confidence in the situation that was unfolding and prevented acceptance of the necessity of impermanence and the ability to change. But, our doubt was gradually chipped away by the events that occurred, including the miraculous blooming of the hollyhocks. While doubt is a normal response that must be gradually reconciled over time, when it is hidden beneath the surface it prevents action and growth, sabotaging all other progress. You must acknowledge the presence of doubt to align it with your heart and spirit then focus on acting without hesitation in the present moment, accepting that nothing is permanent.

TENDING THE PLANET

"The way we live our daily lives is what most effects the situation of the world...
The way we hold a cup of tea, pick up the newspaper or even use toilet paper are directly related to peace."

-Thich Nhat Hanh

This book began with the admonition that learning these 7 Lessons for living from the stories of the dying is crucial to our ability to navigate the future on planet Earth. As we face the uncertainty of looming change and the potential of widespread suffering, we must prepare ourselves not only to cope with disaster, but also to rise above it, creating something new in the process. There is an urgent and growing desire among many individuals to save the planet from environmental destruction, create prosperity and health for mankind, and promote peace among Earth's societies. However, any of us who seek to bring balance to the world must first achieve balance within ourselves. We cannot hope to resolve these global issues with actions that are fragmented, compartmentalized, and inauthentic. To heal the planet, we must begin now to work toward integrity, harmony, and clarity in every aspect of our lives, advancing our consciousness as we grow spiritually.

Actions that arise from your wholeness will be in rhythm with the planet, balanced and occurring at just the right time. Nothing more or less is needed from you as an individual. As you continue to practice in your own garden, planting seeds of awareness and pulling weeds from the shadow, the collective field of all mankind will vibrate with the energy you generate, gradually aligning with the rhythm and creating a harmonious and healing union. Hope resides in your inspiration, the breath of life, as you tend to your own garden day after day. Carry on with diligence, extending love and forgiveness, staying in the present moment, letting go of your expectations and facing your fears. Avoid getting trapped by those things that don't matter, such as materialism, status and superficial beauty, even while you negotiate the details of life in the 21st century. Grow like a tiny plant in your garden—breaking open the seed that houses your potential, pushing up through the soil to find the necessary nutrients, swaying in the sun and the breeze as you show the colors of your delicate blossoms. To grow and simply become yourself is your only task. After all, this growth is, and always has been, the only thing that really matters.

For you are both the garden of hollyhocks and the galaxy of stars.
You are the sand and the wave that washes it away.
You are the light and the darkness.
You are Life and Death.
You are the smallest particle within a single atom and
You are the mysterious expanse of Infinity.
You are the Universe with only one purpose: to manifest the Divine.
You are Creation with only one task: to breathe.
In this present moment, all that matters is to stop . . . and breathe.

WHAT REALLY MATTERS

Suffering opens the doorway to spiritual growth.
Embrace your difficulties with equanimity,
recognizing that they are a gift.

Love illuminates the path that stretches before you.
Let your heart be broken to allow the light of love to
shine through.

Forgiveness removes the obstacles on the path of
spiritual growth.
Hold no resentments as you let go of the past and reclaim
your energy.

Paradise is the space between past and future
where your potential becomes your path.
Dwell in the perfection of the Present Moment.

Purpose unfolds continuously in the Present moment,
creating your path one step at a time.
Manifest your highest potential by being who you already are.

Surrender is conforming your path with the rhythm
of the Divine.
Let go of expectations for the outcome of your efforts.

Impermanence completes your circular path to the Divine.
Face your fear of death, recognizing that death makes
creation possible.

NOTES

PREFACE

[1] http://www.deenametzger.com/

[2] http://www.inventingyourlife.com/

[3] George Lamsa, translator, *The Modern New Testament From the Aramaic*, 1st edition (Marina del Rey, CA: DeVorss & Company, 1998).

[4] Substance Abuse and Mental Health Services Administration. (2010). *Results from the 2009 National Survey on Drug Use and Health: Mental Health Findings* (Office of Applied Studies, NSDUH Series H-39, HHS Publication No. SMA 10-4609). Rockville, MD.

[5] Matthew Herper, "America's Most Popular Drugs." *Forbes.com* 11 May 2010: 1. Web. 24 Jun 2010. <http://www.forbes.com/2010/05/11/narcotic-painkiller-vicodin-business-healthcare-popular->.

[6] J.J. Farrell, *Inventing the American Way of Death 1830–1920* (Philadelphia: Temple University Press, 1980).

[7] Lisa Zamosky, "Choices at the end of life." Los Angeles Times 22 Jan 2010: p. 1. Web. 13 Jan 2011. <http://articles.latimes.com/2010/jan/22/health/la-he-end-of-life-costs25-2010jan25>.

[8] *Adapted from*: Karen Wyatt, "An Integral Approach to the End of Life." *Consciousness & Healing: Integral Approaches to Mind-Body Medicine*, eds. Marilyn Schlitz and Tina Amorok (St. Louis, MO: Elsevier, Inc., 2005).

LESSON 1: SUFFERING

[9] Neil Douglas-Klotz, *Prayers of the Cosmos: Meditations on the Aramaic Words of Jesus*, 1st edition (San Francisco, CA: HarperCollins, 1994), 57.

LESSON 2: LOVE

[10] Ken Wilber, *Grace and Grit: Spirituality and Healing in the Life and Death of Treya Killam Wilber*, 1st edition (Boston, MA: Shambala Publications, Inc., 1993), 401.

[11] Wilber, *op. cit.*, 406.

LESSON 3: FORGIVENESS

[12] http://www.matthewshepard.org.

[13] http://en.wikipedia.org/wiki/Amish_school_shooting.

LESSON 4: PARADISE

[14] George Lamsa, *Idioms in the Bible Explained and A Key to the Original Gospels*, 1st edition (San Francisco, CA: HarperCollins, 1985), 59.

[15] Lamsa, *Ibid.*, 102–104.

ABOUT THE AUTHOR

Dr. Karen Wyatt is a family physician who has spent much of her twenty-five-year career as a hospice medical director caring for dying patients in their homes. The author of *A Matter of Life & Death: Stories to Heal Loss & Grief* and *The Loss & Grief Survival Guide*, Dr. Wyatt has lectured and written extensively on end-of-life issues with an emphasis on the spiritual aspect of illness and dying.

Dr. Wyatt recently retired from medical practice to focus her efforts on *Creative Healing*, a project to explore the integration of spirituality and Western medicine. She lives with her husband, Dr. Larry George, in Silverthorne, Colorado and enjoys hiking, running and cycling in the beautiful Rocky Mountains.

Contact Dr. Wyatt for interviews or public speaking:
karen@karenwyattmd.com

Visit her website and subscribe to her newsletter:
www.karenwyattmd.com